I0087773

A Beautiful Life,
A Dream

LEHLABA SAMUEL SEKGOBELA

A Beautiful Life, a Dream!

Copyright © Lehlaba S Sekgobela 2022
ISBN 978-0-620-95556-0

Cover artwork by Lehlaba S. Sekgobela

I dedicate this book to the person walking in the darkest time of their life right now; stuck and lost somewhere along their life's journey; depressed; feeling as though they would never ever see the light; feeling as though life has no meaning, to you I say: 'With this book I'm stretching out my hand and reaching out to you; please stretch yours back to me, and let us walk together through the dark tunnel into the light!'

Contents

Preface

My name is Lehlaba Samuel Sekgobela. I was born February the 24th 1994 in Tembisa, in the Gauteng Province in Mzansi (South) Africa.

My life had been unappealing from a very early age. As a kid I had a very ugly upbringing. My childhood was filled with hurt, sadness and tears. I suffered due to the people I was surrounded with as a kid. It hurts a lot that most of my suffering was brought upon my childhood life by family!

My relatives and other people mocked me, called me by names, and made laughs of me for who my father was and where he was from. Some of my relatives did not even want me in their homes. They would command me to leave their homes when they felt like it.

People made fun of me for my dark skin complexion. This caused me to have a very poor self-esteem as a little boy. It felt as though I was an alien amongst all the other kids. It made me feel as though I did not belong; as though an outcast, and a reject. This broke my heart into a million pieces.

I witnessed poverty firsthand. I know what it feels like to not have enough, to survive on scraps or to not have at all! I know what it feels like to survive on scraps for food or to go to sleep with an empty stomach.

I remember having to go to school in a torn up school uniform. I know what it feels like, to be dressed up in rags amongst other children who came from privileged families who took good care of their needs and wants. I know what it feels like for someone to make fun of one's serious situation, and what damage it can do to the person psychologically and emotionally!

All the things that happened to me as a child caused my childhood life to be dull. I used to wonder: 'Why my parents would put me in a place which would see me suffer as a kid?' Why would my parents leave me in the hands of those who would cause me suffering? Why would the people who had to love and care for me be the ones to abuse me?

Why would my relatives be the ones to mock me in front of the village when they could have been the ones to turn to, the ones who could have stood by me when other people went on to put me through all the mockery? But I have learned that, people have their own selfish and stupid reasons for the things they do to others, no matter the pain their actions bring upon the next person!

Later in my life I got caught in depression. I was twenty years old when this happened. This had been one encounter in my life which I found hard to believe I could pull through. It felt as though I had reached the dead-end with my life.

I just could not cope, I wanted out of life, and my life almost reached an end at some point and, that could have been by my own hands. But, fortunately and eventually I found my way around the situation and I managed to pull through.

I used to wonder to myself, what did I do to deserve all this? A question I would repeat to myself over and over again. For a very long time, hate and anger raged and boiled inside of me. I pointed a finger and casted blame. I never knew peace because of all the things I went through my whole life.

Yes, I used to wish my parents did not take me to and put me into the place where my childhood would be an unappealing one. I used to wish I could have had the better childhood life and upbringing I deserved as any other kid; and that I was not put through abuse.

I used to wish my relatives did not chase me out of their homes; that people did not mocked me and; made fun of my dark skin complexion and called me by names; that I was never put through all the hell I was put through; and that I had a very different but beautiful experience with my childhood life!

But, the past is something intact and fixed; something which cannot be changed. Even if I wanted to, no matter what I had and have been through; no matter what the world and its people have put me through; no matter the hardships, no matter the heartbreak, no matter the pain and no matter the tears I cried, I would not dare change anything about my past! Trust me I would not dare!

Because, all the things I have and had been through with my life, pushed me to learn life's most crucial lessons; to become wiser and more understanding of life's crucial matters and to become a better individual. You know what they say '*what does not kill you only makes you stronger and wiser*'.

At a very crucial point in my life, the point of depression to be precise, I paused to learn the most crucial lesson regarding this life. I looked at a bird and I envied its way of life; how it cut across the sky with ease; how it appeared to be free and happy. I wondered to myself '*would my life ever be as beautiful as that of the bird?*'

I wondered to myself, 'do birds have abusive families? Do birds have unloving relatives who chase them away from their homes? Do other birds mock them for who their parents are or what the colors of their feathers are? But birds appeared to me to be happy creatures. And I thought 'why not with me?'

I thought to myself, what if someone killed the bird? Right there, I arrived to the most amazing idea regarding this life '*violation and misfortune*'. If someone or any other creature was to kill the bird, this would be pure violation in regard to its life. If it was to be killed in a natural disaster it would only be unfortunate.

This idea made me look at life through a very different sight; a completely rejuvenated sight. I looked at my life and all that I have been through, and imagined if I was born and raised in a different world; a world where people showed me love and respected me as a child and, I had all my needs and wants provided for.

I learned that I was only unfortunate to be raised by and to grow up amidst the people with cruel hearts, people who have failed to respect and show me love. I was only unfortunate to grow under those hurtful situations. Should I had been birthed and raised in a good place, amidst good people I would only have been fortunate.

But a child does not choose by whom and where they wish to be born into this life and world do they? I looked at all the abuse and the mockery I had suffered as pure violation to a kid to have a peaceful, happy and a beautiful life!

Later in life, as a grown up, I asked myself the most precious question. This had been after I had pulled through depression, but my life just did not flow and I had found myself camping in what I referred to as the *'Slum of Misery'*.

I wondered to myself, *if I had a beautiful life,* what would it look like? I wondered to myself if such a life was even possible or was I caught in fantasy of the impossible just because I had an unappealing life? Well, I was looking for the complete opposite of that, the opposite of ugly---***a beautiful life!***

I would go to pen down the idea of a beautiful life and, the idea of *a beautiful life became not just an idea but a divine dream!* The more I dwelled on the idea of a beautiful life; I learned that naturally, like a bird or a flower, to have and live a beautiful life is a natural/birth right! The idea saw me change my life in the most special way!

I learned that *'like a seed which unfolds and grows to become the fully fleshed flower it ought to be'* so shall a person's life unfold in this world, and be what it ought to naturally be---beautiful'. It is a person's natural/birth right, no matter their challenges in life, to have and to live a beautiful life! No one was birth into this world to suffer. No!

No one deserves to go through what I had gone through myself. But who chooses for that innocent kid? But, my past, the things I had been through in life have made me pause and look at life with a careful eye; to observe life better and derive the need to understand what the very matter, this life, is all about.

My past encounters and experiences, no matter how hurtful and painful, they have broken me at one point in my life, but have helped mold me as an individual into a better person; a person who had grown wiser over the years; a person who had learned how to endure, how to be patient, how to be self-loving, how to be understanding, empathetic and caring towards others!

Along my life's journey, I had picked up and learned a whole crucial lot, a crucial lot I believe I could not have picked up nor learned of if I did not go through what I had gone through in my life. From within the egg of my painful experiences I had come out a beautiful soul, I confess! And I had chosen to live my life in the best way possible!

Life is a very difficult thing, happening in a very cruel place, amidst the cruelest of people and painful events! Some seeds just do not have it easy in this life, and within this world. Some find them self having to grow amidst the weeds and, all they have to do is to be strong!

I cannot begin to imagine, how many people had/have to go through what I had been through myself every day, and how that has impacted and continues to impact their life right now. It is an idea very hard to bear at mind. It weighs heavily upon the heart.

My painful experiences have made me derive the need to reach out to others who have been put through pain in life in some way. I have found it a need to reach out to other people, to look into, to discuss and help them cope and deal with such matters which I have experienced myself in my own life.

My experiences have made me fall in love with psychology and sociology. I have fallen in love with the idea of psychology and sociology somewhere along my life's journey. I have learned how crucial the mind is upon our life and why it should be of care priority!

But, I was neither a psychologist nor a social-worker to help anyone in any way psychologically or sociologically professionally. But, it is still my dream to study psychology or social work one day soon, for all the impact I wish to make wholeheartedly is in these two special fields. Maybe sooner or not so late in my life I would get there or, maybe perish upon that journey.

But, I had chosen another special way to try and reach out to and help other people and that is 'writing'. I respect writing. I have always been in love with writing. I am passionate and love the art of writing so much! I have always written stories, poetry and lyrics; so I chose to use the art of writing as the tool and the platform to reach out to other people.

I vowed to myself that, I will not just be a writer, but one who writes passionately with love, expresses freely, with a bountiful of respect and honesty my ideas and a genuine content which would provoke the thought, touch and change the life of the next person!

So, I had put myself to the task of writing this book. I wrote this book to try and reach out to the next person, to provoke their thought, to usher light, to touch their heart and, to inspire change towards having and living a beautiful life!

One does not have to submit blindly to my ideas but, to strive and derive pure sense and understanding out of them. So, I hope one would not only enjoy reading this book, but let the ideas carved within its pages usher light upon some crucial areas of, and help them improve their own life!

Introduction

We all have dreams! We dream of different things; from the tiniest and the simplest of things to the greatest and divine things! We dream of the sensible and the most silliest of things! And there are no set boundaries as to how much we can dream!

Our dreams differ from one individual to another; because we are different people with different perception and preference in regard with this life. But, even with our differences in views and desires, we all share a common dream. And, I see a cloth of wonder wearing your face!

Yes, we all have a common dream. Regardless of how much we may differ in our views with life, we all share the dream of having and living a beautiful life. We may have not realized the idea yet, but we do share this common dream.

If we asked every individual being in the world this question: 'What is it that they wanted with their life?' all the answers would point to the direction of a particular dream and that is, to have and to live a beautiful life!

We may dream of graduating in a particular field of study; to be successful; to have peace; to live a life filled with purpose and meaning; to be loved; to be healthy; pleasant; to make an impact in this life; to be happy; to have the job, the car, the house, the life partner and the family of our dreams; to travel the world; to be a renowned celebrity; and or to go to the moon someday.

All these ideas form part of an individual picture, a single but enormous picture of a divine dream and that is, a beautiful life. All the things we have ever dreamt of, be it freedom, peace, success, financial freedom and independency, bliss or any other thing, all these things are separate parts, but crucial parts which interact and fuse perfectly well to form this one big beautiful dream, the dream of a beautiful life!

At a particular point in time, ten different people may want different things in their life, which is so because not every person is born into this world the same way; into the same circumstances nor would their lives unfold in the same way nor with the same pace as compared to the life of the next person.

One person may want peace at particular time in their life. The other might want financial freedom; the other spiritual or physical healing; to have the woman or the man of their dreams; to have a child or any other sort of dream.

This does not mean that we do not share the divine dream of realizing and living a beautiful life. No! It is just that at a particular moment in life, two or more individuals felt a certain void which needed to be filled in their own life. But all the important dreams mentioned above, all encompasses and form part of this one divine dream!

In this regard, I speak not only for myself, but for the next person too, when I say that, as we 'walk this earth' we all wish to have and to live a flowing, flourishing, abundant, pleasant, and meaningful and a happy and a joyful life! And, that can be reduced to one idea, a beautiful life!

But, as much as we would want to realize and live a beautiful life, life is a very complicated matter, a cryptic and a very complex matter! It is a matter which can prove hard to work sense out of, and to comprehend and further worse, a complicated matter taking place in a very complicated place---our world!

Our world is a very crazy and a very cruel place, with a whole lot happening, a whole lot that whether we believe it or not, like it or not nor want it or not, we will encounter matters, from the simplest to the most cryptic along a life's journey, which would most definitely impact our life in some way!

Life is full of hardships and trials! It is made out of encounters presented to every one of us 'here' in black and white (good/bad). It is like an enormous puzzle, which presents us with a plentiful of challenges we have to walk through; challenges which may stand before us and curb us from realizing the dream of having a beautiful life!

In a life's journey, we all go through the ups and the downs', we meet with humps and curls, with which we toss and we turn; we meet with crossroads, and there we may pause puzzled for some time, not knowing which path to make or take!

We all meet with the steepest up hills to climb and ascend over; a bountiful of obstacles and boundaries, which we have to break through; and we meet with thorns along our path which we have to step through and walk over!

Sometimes we find we have to walk through the dark tunnels designed by particular life challenges! If we were fortunate enough we sooner found our way and managed to walk out the other end. But, if not fortunate, we may find that we have to walk within the dark tunnels of our life's challenges longer than we could have imagined!

Sometimes the challenges we meet with along our life's journey may appear to be bigger than us. They may seem impossible to resolve. We may be held by circumstances, to not be able to resolve them yet. We may feel stuck and lost somewhere along our life's journey and feel like it may forever be so, and that we might never realize freedom, peace, prosperity, and happiness in our life.

But, in the face of our life's challenges, critical and painful as they may be, hard as they may be for us to resolve and to continue to bear, what are we to do? What should we do when we are feeling tired and weary? What should we do when we find that we are hanging by the thin thread of hope? Should we go giving up on our life's journey? It births a crucial question does it not?

What if I told you there was a way out of the dark tunnel? What if I told you there is light at the end tunnel? What if I told you besides the entire life challenges, one could walk out at the other end a whole new person?

What if I told you that after walking out at the other end, one could view their challenges as the refining sources of their life? What if I told you that one could come to realize that the dark tunnels, tough as they may have been, were the corridors to self-growth? What if I told you that, besides all the challenges in life, we could still realize our divine dream in having and living a beautiful life?

Well, please do bear with me as I share with you my own life's story; the story of my life challenges; the up hills and the down hills; the crossroads and the thorns and how they have influenced my life, and how I have gone about to deal with them in pursuit of my dream in having and living a beautiful life.

I   welcome   you   to   'A   BEAUTIFUL   LIFE'

CHAPTER 1

A Beautiful Life

Life is our ultimate and our divine gift, gifted to us by Mother Nature! It is a gift so precious, none in the whole world can be compared with, and none in the whole universe can surpass it, for its value is unparalleled!

Life is something which we had not chosen our self, nor was it in our power to do so. But life is something which had chosen us instead! We had been gifted this gift, not as a result of our own request, for life is a gift that rests upon chance, and it is by chance that we are 'here' right now!

Now that we are 'here', none much really matters! What really matters is that, we had been presented with a gift, and that is---our very own life! What really matters now is how we decide to unfold our gift, which rests entirely upon the black and white in our thought, interpretation, perception, understanding, wisdom, decisions and our behaviors along our life's journey!

Life is a journey between our birth and our death. Somewhere in between the two crucial events, something special ought to happen and that is, to give it our utmost best, and try to unfold our gift in the best way possible. By that I mean, *to live life, truly live this life!*

We had come into this world to experience what a miracle this life is in peace; to come together with others with love, empathy, compassion, humility, humbleness, honesty, trust and respect; to share and express freely one to another our ideas in regard with this life; to work collectively towards the good of all of life and, to live with one another in harmony!

We had come into this world, to live a natural beautiful life, a flowing and flourishing life, a pleasant, purposeful, meaningful, happy and a joyful life, that when our end had come, we would accept it with pure gladness, knowing deep inside that we had witnessed what a miracle this life is, and setting foot 'here' was a divine and the most wonderful experience; and that between our birth and death we honestly and truly lived our life!

Like a seed imbedded in the soil which then unfolds and grows, undisturbed to become the beautiful flower it ought to be, so shall a person's life in this world unfold and be---a beautiful life! It does not matter by whom nor where we were born; it does not matter the color of our skin, our culture or religion or any other possible distinguishing factor there is; what truly matters is that our life in this world is ought to be a beautiful life!

So may it be.

A Beautiful life for me:

It would be an elegant, peaceful, pleasant, purposeful, important, meaningful, flourishing, abundant and a happy life! In this beautiful life I woke up into the day with a smile wearing my face, went out into the world, free and confident; free to be me, the real me!

I did the things I love, the things I am passionate about! I read! I wrote! I spoke! I sang! I recited! Out of passion and love! I helped those in need out of the pure kindness of my heart! With the art of beautiful living---with the waves of love I touched the lives of others in the most important and very special way!

I shared my life with beautiful people---people with beautiful minds and hearts; people who meant well; and they and I cooperated with great humbleness and respect towards the greater good of all life and lived in harmony and peace!

When my end had come, I would welcome it with pure gladness; without any fear or regret, knowing deep in the core that I had exercised my 'Right to have and to live a beautiful life in this world' and that I have lived---truly lived my life!'

CHAPTER 2

Depression

I believe we all go through the ups and the downs in life; we toss and we turn; we reach the steepest uphill's to climb and to ascend over; we meet with thorns along our path which we have to step through and walk over; and sometimes we meet with the crossroads and mazes along our life's journey, and there we pause puzzled for some time before we could work out a path to make or take.

We all meet with encounters and experiences along the way, which influence our life in some way. Today is this, tomorrow is that, black or white, good or bad, life goes as such. It is how our life unfolds and molds in this world. There is no other way around it!

I like any other person, have been through the ups and the downs in my own life. I had tossed and I had turned. I reached and met with crossroads and mazes a several times in my life, which had me puzzled for some time before I could work out what path to make or take.

I reached the steepest up hills which proved hard for me to climb, and to ascend over. I met with thorns along the road which I had to step through and walk over. And I had a plentiful of encounters and experiences, good and bad and, they had a great impact upon my life!

At the age of twenty I got caught in depression. This was the most enormous encounter I had come to face in my whole life; an encounter so cruel and painful that I personally believe that no encounter in life would ever be as cruel and painful as depression can be!

Depression caused me to suffer greatly in all the vital areas of my life! I suffered greatly psychologically, socially, physically and emotionally! My life turned toilsome in all these important corners of life. I suffered automatic negative thoughts, my body felt tired and heavy all the time. I grew isolated and felt emotionally ragged! *Depression turned my world upside down!* My world became all dull and gloomy! I felt as though this dark cloud hung over my head. Thoughts were a congested traffic upon my mind. I could not think straight. I felt enormously confused and, heavily stressed; outdone and overcame by fear; and defeated by automatic negative thoughts, with no bits of might over them!

The depression **threw me around and made me forget who I was, was about and where I was headed with my life**! I lost the sense of self importance, worth, esteem and confidence! In the process, I lost out on a whole lot. I lost out on so many precious opportunities, lost out on other people's funds and most importantly I lost out on so much time!

Depression curbed my life's flow, crippled and delayed my dreams! I lost the inspiration to do the things I love, the things I have always been passionate about, as in writing and doing music. The direction of my life became all blurry and vague. I grew confused and unsure of what I wanted out of this life!

I grew impatient and angry towards myself and towards the world. I forgot what it felt like to be calm and happy. I distanced myself from people, even those who were a beautiful part of my life. I preferred to be isolated---be by myself most of the time.

I hardly spent time with the closest people in my life. My relationship with family and friends suffered greatly. When I was out with others I would become impatient to get back into my own space, be by myself and far from anyone else.

I felt like I did not have a place nor belonged in this world or with anyone. I felt like an alien and an outcast; unwanted and rejected. I felt like the whole world was against me. I felt like every person saw through me, what a mess I was deep inside. I grew pessimistic towards other people. I feared their behaviors could be negative towards me. I just did not trust anyone. I became isolated and lonely!

In the process I developed the fear of hanging around other people. I preferred to be all alone most of the time. I dwelled on thoughts and unending questions like: *'why me? What did I do wrong? What did I do to deserve all this?* I spent most of my time in my room overthinking. I cried over and over, again and again!

During all this, I was in the dark of what was happening to me. An honest fact the next person might find hard to believe. I did not know that I had depression. Not until later. I had a bountiful of questions in my mind about my situation, but I could not work out what was wrong with me.

For some time I thought that I was just stressing over not being able to make it to varsity when I had just matriculated. But, that was not the case. Later I developed the thought that maybe my situation was the result of a curse or; a punishment brought upon me by and from a deity.

Speaking of deities and curses; my situation made me climb mountains at night in prayer, hoping my prayers would ascend to a deity somewhere in a place unknown, and that they would hear my cry, come rescue and set me free from my situation. But, I will not go deep with this. You know what they say: *'A spiritual belief, a person's personal problem!'*

My situation grew ponderous and tough for me to bear with. I grew weary of the psychological, emotional and social pain I endured every day. I felt helpless, to some extend hopeless. I assumed my situation as permanent. I thought that, I would never be fine; that I would never realize peace and happiness as long as I lived.

I developed suicidal thoughts. *'End it! End it all at once and be at peace!'* Depression whispered into my mind. I lost count of how many times I had tried to cease it, I mean, to end my own life. It is countless how many times I had the knife pointed direct to my heart or my belly, ready to run up against the wall.

If anyone could have asked me at that particular time in my life, what was it that I wanted or wished for? I could have simply said to them: *'all I want is peace and happiness!'* Was this too much to ask? Well, depression made me feel otherwise; and totally convinced me that it was pointless for me to stay alive and that, death was my only ticket out of my sorrows!

So many nights I wished I died during my sleep and not wake to my miserable life. I wanted out of this life. Death became a dream. I felt as though, life had chosen me by mistake. Taking my own life would be my ultimate achievement. I would take a missing bullet so that, I stopped living a miserable life. *'Maybe in death I would be at peace at once'* I thought to myself.

The idea of death just revolved in my mind like every day. *'In death I would be free forever'* depression told me. I wished the night could lay me to an eternal peaceful rest, but the dawn woke me up to my miserable life every day. I wished the sun could set with my life, but dawn thought otherwise.

But in the midst of this dark mist; in the den of this terrible experience; within this situation where I was haunted with negative automatic thoughts; overcame by fear and anxiety; confused and stressed; in this turmoil and pain; and in this great slum of misery where my life was all dull and gloomy, and suicidal thoughts dominated my mind, I had something to hold on to.

Hope! Hope in its thinnest voice whispered into my soul: '*Hold on and hold tight dear one… this shall pass one day soon*'. The hands of hope kept pulling me back when I was walking closest to the edges of my life! Hope in its thinnest thread held on to me when I was about to take a fall into the pit of death! Hope made me a coward to take my own life!

Hope kept me alive to see another day! Hope gave me the chance to work out a way around my situation! In that darkest time of my life, hope kept me going. Limping psychologically, physically, socially and emotionally, hope kept me going and I eventually pulled through!

If I was to Describe Depression

I would just shut my eyes, look at myself in that haunting mirror of depression and reflect. I would just say: 'In the state of depression, one feels enormously confused and, heavily stressed! They feel outdone by automatic negative thoughts! In this state it feels as though our head is buried deep in the grey clouds.

Depression has a negative impact upon the most important corners of a person's life. It pulls a person down psychologically, physically, socially and emotionally! It messes them up in these important areas of life. It causes a person to not be able to think clear. The person experiences fatigue in their body. It causes them to grow isolated and lonely. It makes one feel sad and less inspired. Depression causes one to feel empty in the inside; to feel as though there is a big hole in their life which can never be filled; to feel as though one is alone in this world; and happiness is none but like an impatient guest in their heart. With depression everything is just so dull and one just feels sad almost all the time!

Depression diminishes our sense of self-worth, confidence and esteem. The wells of it all become desert dry. The meaning of life escapes our mind, and, hope deserts our heart. We lose the sense of who we are and are about. Our dreams become vague and obscure. Life just seems to have no direction at all but just a spiraling maze.

Depression is a bully! Depression is the most cruelest and ruthless encounter in the whole of life. It is the toughest experience ever! With depression, life is an everyday mental, physical and spiritual toil and drudgery. Life is unpleasant and hard to live. Life is just painful with depression!

Depression pushes us to isolate, to be and to feel alone. The only place we ever go to is in our mind. With depression, one's closest companions seem to be their own negative thoughts, and bitter emotions. All that one ever does when they are alone is cry over and over again.

Depression causes one to seek an escape from reality by tuning their thought or getting lost in games, music, a movie or any other particular task that may help them forget of their situation but, it never does for long because, the depression gravity always pulls them down so hard!

Depression causes one to walk at the edges of their life. I mean, depression can cause one to be suicidal. And, lacking understanding of the matter, or not undergoing necessary treatment might be the contributing factor towards the threat and the absolute ending of one's own life!

When time lapses away, without one having not met with or having not learnt proper and effective ways to deal with the depression, the pressure grows intense. One may find them self feeling as though their life has no meaning; that it is pointless to continue living.

The idea of not finding an effective way/s to deal with the situation may be due to not knowing what the problem is to begin with. It is very much possible. I myself had been caught and gone through depression for three years, with no glimpse of idea of what the problem was. Could it be that I have bunked that one important Life-skills class back in high school? I wonder!

During that period, this harshest period in my life, I have believed that: '*I must have been bewitched. Maybe a supernatural being somewhere in a spiritual dimension, a deity must have brought the situation on me as a form of punishment*'. But it had not been that.

We may find our self stuck in the situation for some time because, we had/have little to no resources to deal with the situation or we did not know of any. For example: resources such as meditation, yoga, affirmation etc. or we had not enough means to afford professional psychological help!

If we did not get any necessary help, we might even begin to lose hope that we could ever beat the depression. We might even begin to assume the situation as permanent. And, also begin to feel as though we would have to live with the situation our whole life.

If we felt as though we do not have the power over the matter nor believe that it could ever be mended, we might even freak out! Our situation might worsen and get overwhelming that, we might sooner or later reach a breaking point!

When we feel as though there is no possible solution to the situation, we might even grow suicidal. We might find our self having ideas about taking our own life or even attempting to do so! Because we feel we cannot take it anymore and, we see death as our only way out. *'End it and be at peace at once'* we might give it thought and, might go trying to or go pulling the plugs!

Having gone through depression and having beaten it myself; knowing how psychologically, physically, socially and emotionally draining it is and can be; knowing how painful and sorrowful it is; how difficult it is to battle with automatic negative thoughts day in and out; how it feels to live in sadness and wetting the pillow with tears at night; feeling helpless and hopeless; and feeling suicidal and wanting to continue living this life at the same time-

Let me tell you this--- hear me: '*Whoa!*' It is not the time to go pulling the plugs yet, or never. Hold on a sec because, it is when the wound is still fresh, which makes it very hard for one to believe the pain could ever go away, but it does eventually! Trust me, it does! Depression is but like a fresh wound. It will try to convince us so hard that it is unbeatable and permanent, that it is here forever to stay.

But, like a pain in a fresh wound, it eventually does in time go away. All it needs is the necessary treatment, to be paid effort and time to heal. *We cannot afford to lose this once off precious gift called life, not to depression! No! We have to fight!*

We must make it our priority and our ultimate goal to beat depression! We must see it as an enemy which is standing before us and realizing a beautiful life, which it is! We must see it as something we had come into this world to conquer; our life's mission and purpose! *We cannot afford to give up! We cannot afford to let depression win!* We got to fight with all that we have!

We have the natural right to have and to live a beautiful life in this world! A beautiful life it has to be as long as we are still kicking! We cannot allow depression or any other cruel encounter violate this right, because, beyond the walls of depression, there is a beautiful life that awaits us. It is only that depression blinds us to see how beautiful our life ought to be, and could be!

Yes, depression is painful, but depression can be the most refining encounter and experience. From within the flames of the hells of it we can crawl out refined, rejuvenated and beautiful souls beyond measure! Get the saying: *'Diamonds made in the rough?'* I bet you do.

CHAPTER 3

In The Battle with Depression

One needs to be in the light and to know precisely what the matter is, in order to be able to deal with it. Being in the dark of what the matter is or might be can have us guessing and wondering in confusion. It can cause us to get lost or stuck somewhere along our life's journey!

It was only after learning that I had depression that I had gotten able to deal with it! Being in light of the matter helped me a great deal lot! It helped me drop the thought that I might be cursed or suffering a punishment brought upon my life by a supernatural being/s! All the guessing, wondering and confusion ceased! It was no longer as though trying to catch a fly in the dark!

The quest towards finding the solution to my problem was important and very special. I had picked up a whole crucial lot along the way, a whole crucial lot which I believe is pretty much basic, and very simple to ignore without realizing how crucial it is in regard with living this life!

My journey towards beating depression began with me fiddling about on the internet and reading more about it. I read just about anything I bumped upon on the internet related to depression. This helped me learn and understand the matter a little bit deeper!

Although I was not looking to build deeper knowledge on the matter, but rather to find the solution to it, I saw the need to have enough understanding of what I was dealing with, which meant that I had to learn more about the matter itself!

In fiddling about for ways to deal with the depression, I have learned that, the ways are very basic and very crucial for a healthy life. They are the foundation to, and form a bridge between the self and a healthy lifestyle!

There are a few ways to choose from to deal with depression. One can get professional help from a doctor, a psychologist, and psychiatrist; undergo self-treatment or see any other relevant personnel who would be of help, maybe a monk or a spiritual guru, who knows?

I, myself have undergone self-treatment in beating depression. It was not an easy way. It was very difficult, but a very crucial path. I got to learn a whole important lot on the road which has helped me to heal, and to grow in the crucial areas of life, mentally, physically, spiritually, emotionally and socially!

The path I took, I mean self-treatment, was not simple at all! The path required a whole lot of effort. I had to make enormous adjustments in all the crucial areas of my life! Discipline and sacrifice were a must! There was no other way, no easy way and no shortcuts!

But all the discipline, effort, time and the sacrifices I poured into the self-treatment process, in applying and putting into practice the ways which proved tough, I managed to pull through at the end! All the everyday hard work yielded great results. I witnessed rain pour down into the desert of my life, and cause it to grow into the sea upon which my life's boat came to float enabling me to row!

Visualizing Victory

On the road towards beating the depression, I visualized my destination! I visualized life beyond the depression! I would shut my eyes, and I would see myself walking out into the light at the end of the tunnel, free of depression and happy!

The picture at mind was so vivid and clear to my mind's sight, so vivid and alive it felt as though I had arrived there already! I longed for healing wholeheartedly that, nothing in the whole world, nothing at all, mattered to me as much as beating depression did at that particular point in time!

'What sort of life would I live after I had gotten past this painful experience?' I paused at one point during the journey in depression, and wondered to my desperate self. *'I would strive to cultivate and live a tranquil and a very joyful life!'*

'I would respect my peace! I would never do or allow anything or anyone to cause me unrest or interfere with my peace! Never, ever! I would strive to be happy no matter the odds! And, I would value and cherish my peace and happiness beyond measure!'

This helped me stay hopeful, optimistic, strong, disciplined and to persevere throughout my journey in dealing with the depression! I was immensely hopeful at heart that I would eventually make it through the dark tunnel of depression and realize peace and happiness!

Talking To Someone

I had always been one not to open up or to be transparent to anyone about my deep personal and private matters! I never really had someone who I would go to with my problems. So, I had always shelved my problems in the inside! This had always made life very hard for me!

After learning that I had depression, I found it very difficult to mention or to talk to anyone about it. Besides not really having that someone in my life that I could trust with my private matters, I felt ashamed and afraid! I don't know why but, I just felt ashamed to share my problem with the next person!

I had the thought that the next person might not get me, they might not understand. I felt as though I would appear weird and give the next person the reason to judge or ridicule me. So, I found it, if I said *a bit* I would be underestimating it, but honestly speaking, rather very hard to talk about my problem to anyone!

As I reflected upon my past, I realized that something important, something special inside of me had broken when people have put me through pain in the past. So *I had lost faith and lacked trust in people!* Something I had to deal with later!

I just went on to face the situation all by myself! I underwent self-treatment to avoid having other people intervene in the matter. It had not been an easy process though, but the pain brought upon my life by the depression just gave me a great push to work even harder!

Someone to talk to or not, I wanted out of the depression as in yesterday, and I was willing to go through it all by myself! So, my journey through the dark tunnel of depression had been a very lonely one but not entirely! But, I managed to pull through.

Even so, I believe my journey through the depression could have been a bit much easier, if I had someone walking with me. Although I had pulled through at the end, I had learned the hard way that, one should talk to someone about their problems.

Not everyone is an enemy! Not every person is out to hurt us like those who had! There are still good souls out there, beautiful souls with beautiful hearts; people who mean well and would, out of compassion and love walk with one every step of the way through their life matters.

It helps to know that we are not alone, especially in the toughest moments in our life. That is why it is of crucial help to open up and be transparent with our problems to those we trust. Because, at the end of the day, it is in knowing that someone knows, someone cares and they are supporting us, that we stand strong in the midst of all the storms encountered upon our life's journey!

Taking Care of the Body

All my life I never really took good care of my body. I never really had a healthy diet, took out time to exercise or had a healthy sleeping habit! I never exercised! I would eat and drink just about anything with a good taste! I would stay up passed the midnight hour or worse, till the cock croaked in the morning, and woke up feeling fatigued!

For as long as I can recall, physically my health had always been very poor! I had always felt bad of my poor self-administration. I suffered greatly the effects of the continuous habits I had built over time!

To sum it all up, although it is hard to admit but an honest fact, I would say that, *what reflected from my poor behavior were pure self-destruction, disrespect and lack of self-love!* A bitter pill to swallow but pure truth!

Because, to take care of the self in any crucial area of life, be it mentally, physically, spiritually, emotionally, or socially, reflects pure self-respect and love! To neglect and fall short of care on these vital areas of life leads to pain and suffering!

In trying to remedy my situation, inspired too by the idea that it would help me in healing from depression, I pushed myself to make compromises and great adjustments to improve my physical health.

In not so long, although it was very hard to, I decided to play the hell away from any form of processed intake and practiced healthy eating, although none much was there. I made sure that all that I took into my body was purely healthy, no excuse!

I decided to adopt and put to practice a healthy sleeping habit! I gave up all the unnecessary crap which made me stay up at night, when I should be sleeping and resting my precious body!

I had put myself to the challenge of **respecting the sleep and the wake**; I mean my sleeping and waking up time. I pushed myself to sleep around 8pm every night and wake up around 4am in the morning!

My sleeping time allowed me to get enough sleep and body rest. Waking up around 4am worked wonders with me! *I deeply respect that time of the morning!* Arriving early into the day just made me feel in control and, allowed me to prepare for the day ahead of me and approach life with great enthusiasm!

As for body workouts, I had no ideas of what to do about that at first. I wanted something simple but effective at the same time. I was looking for the sort of workout which would make my body feel lighter. I wanted an exercise which would allow me to work out my body without using any supporting objects.

I searched and I searched and came across one of the most amazing workout in 'Kundalini yoga'. Each morning I would wake up and practice Kundalini! It was not an easy task but, with discipline and effort, I got a hang of things! Although I backslid sometimes, I kept going!

At the end, I would realize great improvement in my physical health! My body came to feel lighter and brighter with each morning! And, all the care I had given to it played a very enormous role in me healing from depression!

Taking Care of the Mind

The mind is a very crucial aspect of our life. It allows us to be aware of the things around us, to think and to feel. From it a very powerful source is born and that is our thought, which is the source of our actions and behaviors!

Without the mind, thought cannot take place. If thought cannot take place then action cannot be possible. We do not have to dive deep into the philosophy of '*the workings of the mind*' in order to understand this, because it is pure basic sense!

Everything that we do in our everyday life is so as the result of the workings of our mind, how we think. We think of everything prior to action, from the simplest and the tiniest things such as blinking our eyes, to the most critical and enormous things such as solving mathematical equations.

But one needs a sober and positive mind to be able to steer their life. Because, what we think can either mold or break our life! Apart from the occurrences we have no power over in life, how our life turns out at the end becomes so as the result of our actions, which are the results of our very own mind. You know what they say: **"A positive mindset, a positive life!"**

For us to best steer our lives, that towards the right direction, we need to be of calm and sound mind. We need our thoughts to be in the purest state as best as possible! Because, it is of the sound mind and purest thoughts that we would be able to best navigate and mold our lives in this world.

But, we are living in a critical world. Our life as humanity is taking place in a very crazy world! A whole lot is happening in our world with every bits of it almost entirely negative! We are exposed to too much negative events and information which in turn influence the way we think in our everyday life!

The negativity may be passed on to us by those around us in self or somewhere far across the world;   through social media and networks! We may pick up the negative information from the simplest of ways; from the negative claim by a broadcaster on the television; a remark on the radio; a comment on Facebook or Twitter; a negative scene in a movie or series; or a negative content in a song!

All the negativity may interfere with and cause us unrest at mind! It may cause it hard for us to focus and be able to steer our lives as best as we could! We may find that, the negativity steals our calm and focus in doing the crucial things which are to mold our life for the better!

How then can we keep calm and be of sound mind, and of the purest thought in the midst of all the negativity in the world? How can we keep our minds calm and focused? How can we channel our thought towards doing the important things which ought to be done in order for us to realize a beautiful life? How can we stay positive in a world ruled by negativity?

Honestly, there is always a way around every matter! Just because we do not know of any, yet, that does not mean that there is no way at all! It is always after finding the particular way to deal with a matter that we realize, the resolve had always been in our reach! But, just because we did not know, we thought there was never any to begin with!

Meditation

There I was one beautiful day, in my room, sitting on the chair, headphones wearing my ears, passionately listening to and following the voice of one of the most amazing souls in the world, the voice of **Deepak Chopra**.

'Sit comfortably; feet planted firmly on the ground; your back against the backrest; relatively erect; your feet uncrossed; your hands open like my hands are; and close your eyes. With your eyes closed observe your breath as it goes in and out through your nostrils. Do not manipulate your breath; and do not try to change it. Just observe it; you will see it slows down. Tell yourself; let my mind become one with my breath. Just continue observing it, with your eyes closed, for about three minutes.'

What was I doing here; sitting on the chair with my eyes shut, following the voice of a man in the video I just bumped upon not so long? What was this about observing the breath without manipulating it, and telling myself: *'Let my mind become one with my breath?'* What in the world was this about?

Well, this was the most precious practice which would soon change my life in the most amazing but crucial way. *Meditation!* If there is somewhere I would rather be in the whole world, that would be somewhere in a quiet undisturbed place, my body relaxed and my mind floating in meditation. *I could stay here forever I tell you*!

We observe a whole lot with our senses every day. We see, hear, touch and feel a lot. There is a whole lot of information that goes by in the world, which we pick up mostly with our eyes and our ears like every day. And then a whole lot of processing takes place in our minds.

With the whole lot information we take into mind every day, our mind is then left with a whole lot of processing to do. To some extend and or limitation, our mind just cannot handle the pressure of all the thought processing it has to go through!

We find that, we want to focus, but the mind just jumps from one thought to another. The mind begins to chatter! This causes stress! We find that it is very difficult for us to focus! Then it becomes hard to steer our lives!

It ends up feeling like we have no control over our mind, which would mean that we had no control over our lives. It is like we are puppets to our thoughts. This might lead to a great damage in the important areas of our lives! And surely this is something we would not prefer!

But what can we do to keep the mind calm and focused; to stay in control of our thoughts and remain able to steer our lives towards a preferable palatable direction? Well, there can never be any better way for one to be able to calm the mind if not with the practice of **meditation**!

Through the dark tunnel of depression, I had learned of and applied the practice of meditation to my life! This improved my life in a very enormous, and the most precious way! For the first time in my life after some time and effort in the practice of meditation, I became able to pause and look at things with an open mind. I grew calmer; my focus increased; and my patience improved!

In conjunction with the effort I had put in physical exercise, prayer, affirmation and all the other important exercises, my life grew calmer and calmer at mind with each passing day! I felt brighter and lighter! The dark cloud I used to feel was hanging over my head began to dissolve away. I felt in control of every inch of my whole life!

Prayer

It is a religious world our world; a world guided by belief; a world of believers and worshipers. It is a world of so many spiritual beliefs scattered all over. We come from and belong to a variety of beliefs. We pass our faith, we worship, pray to and offer sacrifices to particular deities.

Some people believe in a God/s, some in Godess/s, Allah, Buddah or any other deity. We do so as a result of what we may have been taught, or as a result of our own preference. But at the end of the day, it is all about what one prefers and what works for them personally!

There is no obligation for one to pass their belief to a particular supernatural being. Every person has the freedom of will to decide what to believe in or what not to; because **a person's spiritual belief remains a person's personal problem!**

Why do we have to pray? We pray because, the self is not limited to the physical being, but an extension of the spiritual being. As we walk earth, the body is guided by the mind which is a spiritual matter; a spiritual matter which ought to be guided too.

Prayer helps us communicate with our spiritual guides/deities. It is from the very guides from whom we seek and gather not only the crucial wisdom or the strength to deal with the matters at hand, but to remain positive, hopeful and confident in the face of all the particular matters in regard with our everyday life!

Prayers, to the most crucial extend, like the practice of affirmation (our next topic) plays an important role in our thought, in the way we think. Prayer to some extend improves our focus! When we pray to our spiritual guides with devotion, we do so because of faith, the faith we have on a particular deity!

With the important things we say in prayer, in repetition **(Important note: Repetition)**, a multiple times in a single day, our minds pick it all up, and our thought dwells on it. Because, when we pray about the things we want wholeheartedly, be it healing, protection and other blessings, we do not only draw hope for things to be well, or the power to keep going even when the going is at its toughest, but at the same time **we train our mind to dwell on the positive and important ideas we are praying about**, unknowingly most of the time!

I have prayed throughout my journey in depression, and I testify that, prayer played a vital role in my healing. I testify that prayer is one of the most powerful tools which can help us break our negative thought patterns, improve our positivity at thought and help us cope in the midst of all the negativity which is taking place around us every day! Prayer helped me to stay positive and to have faith that I would defeat depression!

Affirmation and Countering Thought

'It is not something we were born with; it is not a natural behavior for us to be negative minded. It is something we have picked up somewhere along the way in a life's journey. Sooner or later we find ourselves drowning in the sea of our own negative thinking. Then lifr becomes painful to live because of our negative thought patterns!'

'*But negative, is not how our thought should be! No! We have learned to think negative, and we excelled in doing so! But now is up to us to learn otherwise! It is up to us to wash away and purify our thought! It is a wrong which stands to be corrected; a God damn wrong to right away if we are to be of a calm and positive mind!*' One wise young man once said!

How then do we right this wrong? There is no other better way to do that than through the practice of '**affirmation and counter-**

thought!' Since negative thinking is something we had learned, so could we learn how to think positive! All we have to do is to practice substituting our negative thoughts, and tuning our mind upon and affirming on positive ones!

It is not an easy task to practice substituting our negative thoughts, affirming and dwelling on positive thoughts at first though; because, we had learned to think and to dwell on negative thoughts for a long time. So, to practice positive thinking will require much great effort and time!

If we practice thought substitution and affirmation constantly, by bits our mind learns to dwell on positive thoughts, and gets used to it as it has previously with negative thoughts. If we keep telling the self that we can, we indeed can! But if we constantly kept dwelling on the idea that we cannot, we end up failing, worse without trying!

Through the dark tunnel of depression, I had learned to affirm and substitute my negative thoughts with positive ones. In the going of time, the practice had helped me to tune my mind on positive ideas! It helped me stay positive and remain strong and optimistic!

Instead of thinking: '*I don't feel like exercising. I am weak.*' I would go like: '*How refreshing it would be after all the exercise and a hot bath!*' Instead of entertaining the idea that I could never beat depression, I went like: '*I was not born with depression; I can and I will beat it. Yes I will! I will win!*' In doing so I realized that I remained optimistic and strong and this helped me deal with and pull through the depression!

Love and Passion

Doing the things we love and are passionate about, is very powerful in leading a beautiful and a happy life! Because, the things we love and are passionate about are the things we find pleasure and happiness in doing!

We are likely to find that we are good at doing these things because of the love and passion we have for them! We can do these things at any given time. We can go to sleep late doing them, or wake up early in the morning just because we cannot wait to do them! Time seems to fly when we are at it with these things; not with the aim of devouring time away, but because we are devoted to and we enjoy what we are doing wholeheartedly!

The things we love and are passionate of and find pleasure and happiness when doing give us the feeling of self-actualization and worth; they give meaning and purpose to and make our lives beautiful and very special! Because, the true self and purpose reflect best upon the things we love and are passionate of!

Our love and passion can be in art. It can be in reading, writing, music, painting or any other specific form of art; or we can find love and passion in serving any other special purpose; which can be in being a spiritual doctor, a professional doctor in medicine, a police officer, a teacher or any other type of job, because we just love and are passionate about helping other people!

When we start doing the things we love honestly and are passionate of, this improves our psychological well-being! We find that our mind is calmer; because it is occupied in doing the things we love and are passionate about! Our mind is not attracted to negativity, and we do not go dwelling in negative thinking!

In my journey through the dark tunnel of depression, I had pushed myself to do the things I love and are passionate about. I wrote and read more! This provided an escape route from all the overthinking I had going within my mind. In reading and writing I found sanctuary! In the reading and writing I always tapped into and dwelled in this beautiful world of my own.

Instead of taking in too much negative information, or dwelling upon negative ideas which arose at mind, I had my focus upon writing or buried in a book. This helped keep my mind occupied; to not go wondering in negativity and remain focused!

Taking In Inspiration

We intake liquids and food into, and feed our body every day. Our body intake can be good or bad for our health. If our intake is healthy our body gets nourished, we stay healthy and our health improves. But, if the intake to our body is unhealthy, the opposite happens!

Our minds like the body reacts to our intake in information. The information that we feed our minds every day can be good or bad for our mental health; it can influence our thought in a big way, good or bad, but in a very enormous way!

If our information intake to mind is positive, this helps us in staying inspired. But, if our intake to mind is negative, this can cause unrest at mind, a great deal of stress, emotional pain, derail us and pull us down in life!

It is not a joke that **we are living in a world where negativity outweighs positivity!** If we took a pause and took a careful look, paid it mind and analyzed it, we would realize this fact. Too much negativity is going on in our world every day; too much it is easy to notice. I bet even a newly born baby can tell!

This gets thrown and passed around as mentioned earlier, through the social media platforms and networks. It can be that advert during a commercial break on television about a cosmetic product used to brighten up the skin complexion, which in turn causes the next person to feel restless with their natural dark skin complexion!

It may be that negative content of a song playing on the radio, or in our playlist with a dope beat and a negative lyrical content mumbled by a foolish and an inconsiderate '*wannabe*'. It may be that negative post on social media. Get where I am going with this? Thank you!

But, Instead of paying our mind to all the negativity which is going around, we can choose otherwise. We can choose to be cautious or abstain from taking into and paying mind any sort of negativity at the first place!

A whole lot is happening in the world already; a whole lot which we can pay mind. There are natural and orchestrated events taking place like, every day! We have a life to mold! We have dreams; dreams which need us to be calm at mind and stay inspired in order to fulfill them! Why then should we bother paying mind to any negativity passed around when we can avoid it, and tune our minds to the beautiful things going on around us?

For us to feed our thought with negative information is adding an unnecessary thought burden. It causes disturbance and unrest! It creates boundaries which halt us from getting to where we want to get to with life! We just cannot afford negative intake to the mind, if we are to realize peace of mind, and move forward in life!

We can choose to view inspirational content on our television and on our phone screens. We can choose to read something inspiring, in a magazine or paper, or on the net instead of reading negative posts on social networks. We can add to our playlist the type of music which lifts our spirits up!

Taking in positive information is purely healthy for our life. It does not only help us stay inspired, but also helps us build knowledge around other important matters; helps improves our wisdom to deal with matters in certain crucial areas of life!

Through the dark tunnel, I had learned to intake in a whole lot of positivity to mind. I watched a whole lot of inspirational videos. I gave a good ear to the sort of music which uplifted me. I did the things I am in love with and are passionate about as in reading and writing. This played a very crucial role in developing and improving the positivity in my life!

I had realized, one does not always have to be there in person to play a role in the next person's life. One can still reach and touch the next person's life in the most special way! I wanted to believe that my journey through the dark tunnel would be entirely lonely.

But, in not so long I bumped across the most precious souls. Although I have never met them, yet to or maybe never, their beautiful work have played, still do play and even going forth with this life I believe will still play a crucial role in my life!

Some people do walk with us spiritually if we want, and allow it to be so. They may not know it. But, the work they put out there reaches and changes other people's lives in the most beautiful way! This may be so in the form of the art, be it music, poetry, a book, inspirational videos, or any other form of art.

In all the inspirational souls I have bumped across, one stood out for me personally, and that is **Richard Williams aka Prince EA**! He one of the amazing people whose work and ideas in the art of spoken word poetry and motivational videos have touched and helped to change my life in a great way!

I came to know of Prince EA when I had bumped across his spoken word poem '**Can We Auto-Correct Humanity**' a poem about how technology/the digital world has pushed us further and further away from humanity!

From there since, I had fallen in love with, admired and had cosmic respect for his work. **Right there, right there' I knew I had found someone to look up to, a role model!** I have looked up to and drawn inspiration from him ever since! I had never met the **Richard Williams**; but his beautiful work has played a very great and a special role in my life.

Some souls are just so precious and very rare to come by in life. Some people are just a gift to this life; the rarest souls this world could ever have; precious beyond measure! The things they do are just so special! What they do inspires! What they do touches, changes and saves lives! Richard Williams is one of those beautiful souls!

His words: *'This too shall pass!'* echoed in my mind and uplifted me throughout my situation! It had been of his words too that I believed that I soon would beat the depression!

From his work I have drawn the greatest knowledge and wisdom! His work has led to me changing my perception on the word *'Celebrity'*. I have realized that celebrity is a very crucial word, which carries a deeper meaning.

It is a title which does not fit just about any person, but those special individuals who do the most precious things like Richard Williams and any other beautiful people out there do for the betterment and wellbeing of all of life, who ought to be celebrated! So said, it is very crucial to be cautious of the information we are exposed to, and end up taking into mind; because, at the end of the day, the very information will have a great impact upon our thought; and our thought over our life!

Interacting With Other People

I have always been an introvert; always been one to spend much time by myself. But, as much an introvert I am, I had always hung around with and had fun with friends. But, when I sunk deep into depression, I became more than just an introvert, but too isolated. I hardly hung around with my friends or anyone else. This did not feel right at all!

Through the dark tunnel of depression, I pushed myself to go and hang out with friends. During the early days, it was very tough. But, in the run of time, I found myself hanging out with other people without feeling like walking away and wanting to be all alone. I interacted more with other people. And this helped me down the road towards beating depression!

Light at the End of the Tunnel

It had been out of the **willingness and the determination** to win; out of the hunger inside of me, the hunger for freedom, freedom from depression; that I had put in all the hard work, the sacrifices, effort, , and stood firm and disciplined although it was difficult to, every day, to be free!

I had pushed myself **to visualize and affirm on victory; to take care of my body; go to sleep early at night and get enough sleep and rest; to wake up early in the morning; to do fitness exercises; practice positive thinking; meditation; affirmation; do the things I love and are passionate of; to socialize;** all of it in order to win against and be free of depression and enjoy life!

A tough rough road it was, the road towards beating the depression! The going had gone tough so many times I wanted to give up! But, I kept going! Because living with depression is painful and hard! I wanted to be free! I would go to the end of the world for it!

It had been a long difficult journey through the dark tunnel of depression! But somewhere along the way, I began to see the light from the distant, light at the end of the tunnel, which I would walk into later, free of depression at long last!

Through **faith, hope and persistence**, I walked my journey through the dark tunnel. I made it through to the other side, and walked into the light!

If I had managed to beat depression, so can the next person!

CHAPTER 4

A Not So Beautiful Life

IN THE SLUM OF MISERY

Yesterday,
I stare into that of mine,
Unappealing is the picture of an *ugly* past,
Streaming away into forever,
I fiddle with the picks of mind,
The spades of thought,
Hoping to find something there,
But there's nothing,
I turn to hear the echoes of mockery,
Swearing and belittling,
I return into 'the now'
Guilt is starring back at my face,
Regrets overflow the brims of my heart,
I'm torn apart, drowning in the lakes of sadness,
I am a miserable man camping in the slum of misery!

Upon the walls of my mind,
Sketched is a ragged picture of a perfect dream-
Painted with the brushes of fantasy and imagery,
Drawn nearest to the eyes of my subconscious,
For imagery and fantasy are binocular,

A BEAUTIFUL LIFE, A DREAM

My heart dance with elation,
To the tunes and ululations unheard,
The rhythms and vibes of a perfect dream unrealized,
But the unconscious mind-
Knows no black and white between fantasy and reality!
As I Stare at the clock upon the walls of my mind,
Time is ticking away waving '*bye*' in the distance,
I wish I could ask it to wait on me,
I forget time knows no wait!

I shut my eyes and enter the theatre of my mind,
A scene astonishing and mesmerizing meets my eye,
I want to sing a beautiful song,
But my voice deserts me,
I want to give a good divertimento,
But my body denies me motion,
Everything is beginning to catch flames,
My life's stage is crumbling,
Tears fill my eyes and my sight is all blurry,
I can see the audience in the auditorium of my thought,
But no one seems to care,
The inner self is silently crying,
My inner voice is yelling '*get the hell out of here*',
My life's act seems to be reaching an inevitable-
An end without a beginning,
Fear erupts within my heart as though an angry volcano,
My core is a boiling pot of bitter emotions,
Bitter emotions which toss everything up as though a cyclone,
Fear whispers ugly tales of discouragement,
Anxiety narrates stories of illusion,
The low esteems of self devour away my courage,

A BEAUTIFUL LIFE, A DREAM

The wells of my heart overflow with the lava of despair,
I am overcame by hurt,
Tormented by blame,
Outdone by anger,
Misguided by hate,
It feels as though I am losing it, as though I am crazy,
'Maybe I am' it feels so!

No one knows but, I feel stuck and lost,
Somewhere between an ugly past and an unknown future-
Forever arriving,
Hanging by the thin thread of hope in the miserable now,
Walking all alone in the darkest time of my life,
With a dying candle of the spirit-
Mourning a dying dream,
'A beautiful life',
The stepping stones towards my dreams seem to have disappeared-
Deep into the streams of my shallow miseries!
I am skating upon the thin ice of courage,
Walking carelessly upon the edges of my life,
Starring into the pit of my own death,
I think,
Maybe I came 'here' to witness life with my eyes,
Because I am walking earth not living,
'Dead living' amongst the living,
To waft between my birth and my death,
And To die a life unlived!
Well,
How long does it take to mend one's disfigured life?
How long shall one stare at the clock upon the walls of their
hurtles?

How long shall one walk within the dark tunnel of their mind?
How long shall one remain lost in the maze of their own thought?
How long shall one wonder within the sandstorms in the dessert of
their path?
How long shall one live their life in misery?
What does it take for one to realize a beautiful life?
Care to tell me?
?

Poem By: Author.

'How in the world did I end up here?' I wondered to myself, once upon a not so beautiful life. By *'here'*, I meant nowhere! My life had not been the version of what I had long dreamt of. I had not gotten far with this life as I had always dreamt I would!

It was my dream that, at the age of twenty-five I would have my life all figured and sorted. I dreamt that at this age I would have reached my dream in attaining a degree; would be working and earning good! I would invest in my writing career and publish my work. I would have all the other things I always dreamt I would have. All with my life would just be well!

But, I did not make it there, yet! My life's journey had been filled up with a whole lot of U-turns' and detours, which have delayed me from arriving at my dream. The dream which would be reduced to nothing and vanish away as though a slumber dream!

It feels like only yesterday that, I had been in varsity, a student determined to procure a degree in Bachelor of Commerce in Economics. There and then, my life seemed to have a clear direction. The future seemed all vivid and bright! But, things would turn out bad for me, and life would become toil after dropping out of the university!

I would grow past the age of twenty-five, without having achieved anything with my life and it would hurt a lot! At the age of twenty-seven, my life would be on the ground still, not the reflection of what I had long dreamt of! I would be caught somewhere between an unappealing past, a miserable 'now' and fantasies about a beautiful tomorrow!

It had been like, I had shut my eyes for a sec, only to open them and find, six years of my life have disappeared, all of it gone, without a trace, gone with none good from it, none good that my life turned out miserable!

I would take a glance at my whole life, and witness an ugly past flowing away into forever. I looked at my current life, it was ugly! I would peep into the future, but the picture appeared all misty and blurry!

I found myself drowning in misery! No matter how much I tried to keep my head above the clouds, my thought just got pulled deeper into the grey! I stressed a lot because of my situation that I feared I might sink back into depression when I had worked so hard to be free!

No matter how much I had tried to work a way around to get to my dreams, all routes seemed to be blocked! The stepping stones seemed to have disappeared into the waters! All ladders seemed to have worn up and broken! All the ropes seemed to have snapped! And, the bridge towards my dreams seemed to have broken and collapsed!

'Why the hell is I not on the other side, on the other end of this bridge, on the beautiful side?' **I had to pause and introspect!**

After a very deep self-introspection, I learned that there were still much that needed great attention; much which stood to be resolved if I were to realize a beautiful life. I have gotten stuck and lost in life and found myself camping at the slum of misery for some obvious and basic reasons.

I thought to myself that after depression life would be a walk in the park, but I was entirely wrong! There was a whole lot that needed to be done. There were other weeds in my life which needed my attention. **I struggled financially. I was fearful. I held on to the past. I compared myself with other people. And, I had a very poor social life.** I had to make huge decisions and enormous adjustments in regard with these matters!

Because these particular problems were the ones which interfered with my peace and made it very hard for me to think and see things clear with my life. And they were still the ones which caused me to not make any progress with my life.

In dealing with these problems, I had used a very special problem solving procedure which I refer to as 'THE MIND OVER MATTER APPROACH'. It is a very simple, but a very powerful approach which was inspired by the professional Mzansian rapper and songwriter, Siphelele Mnyande known by his stage PdotO. It simply deals with working out what the matter is and finding the solution to the matter.

I personally believe that if a person did not know what the matter was or they decided to leave the matter unresolved, that matter would press and cause difficulties with their life. But, if one knew or paused to work out what the matter was and found the solution to the particular matter, this would work well for their life.

The Mind over Matter Approach

1.   **IDENTIFY THE MATTER**

If we are to resolve a matter, we first need to know what that particular matter is. We cannot be able to resolve a matter without knowing what it is. It is entirely impossible to do so. It will be like trying to find answers without any valid questions. This may cause a lot of wondering and confusion. It will be like trying to hit a bull's-eye of an unknown target in complete darkness, which is impossible.

Some matters may be hard for us to pinpoint whilst some may be easy to. We just got to conduct deep self-introspection to identify what the matter may be. We got to work on flipping the switch to see things clear.

2.   CREATE A GOAL

Every journey has a destination. In the process of resolving a matter we need to know what it is that we want to achieve at the end. The best thing to do in creating a goal would be to draw a clear picture of our life without the particular matter. This will provide a clear objective in regard with resolving the matter.

3.   WORK OUT THE CAUSE

We derive the need to fix a matter because we can feel and see that it is not affecting our life in a good way. *'But nothing comes from nothing'* one smart person once said. There must be a cause to the matter to begin with. We must ask our self where the matter comes from. We need to do this, because to resolve any matter we got to get to the root of it and make adjustments, taking the root of the matter into account. This will help us in dealing with the matter more effectively, and not having to find the very same matter starring back at our face in future.

4.   FIND SOLUTIONS

Problems are unique. They differ in size and difficulty. It may be easy to find solutions for some matters, but difficult for some.

Some problems may have many solutions, but some may have a limited few. But a cure is still a cure, because it cures a particular ailment.

5.   CHOOSE AND IMPLEMENT A SOLUTION

Nobody knows the self better than the self itself. In resolving a matter in regard with our life, we need to go with what we prefer, what suits us and most importantly what feels right at heart. But we need to go with what will work in resolving the matter. Because it is not just about doing it, it is about doing it right so that we can achieve our goal at the end.

6.   MONITOR PROGRESS

After putting our solution to action, we should monitor if there is change, if any progress is being made. We have to be patient though. Because, it may take a pill a couple of minutes to heal a headache, but it may take a severe treatment and more time to heal a severe ailment. If the solution is working, it is good news. If it is not working, we will have to find another better solution for the matter.

CHAPTER 5

Broke

It is an economic world our world, a world driven by the use of money as the most crucial aspect of exchange for our needs and wants in our everyday life! We make use of money to attain just about anything, be it a need or want!

Without enough money or no money at all, it is very difficult for one to get by in life! Life can prove to be very difficult as the cost of living is critically high! It makes no wonder that every person in the whole world is up on their feet and out toiling every day to earn money in order to sustain their livelihoods or even better, to have and enjoy all the financial freedom they can have in this crazy economic world!

Once upon a not so beautiful life, I was dead broke! I had no job which meant I had no sustainable income. I had not even a single penny written to my name. The situation, I mean being broke formed a great bridge between me and my dreams!

I needed money to publish my books, but I just did not have any to do so. I wanted to go to studio; to stand behind the 'microphone' and do what I love, but I could not afford studio sessions. I wanted a breakthrough in life, but almost everything I wanted to do just need money!

The lack of money stood before me and the most crucial things I was in need of, never mind the wants! In some crucial way and to the most crucial extend the lack of money made it hard for me to even afford the basic things I needed to build the foundation towards getting employment or using my talent in writing to earn myself a decent living!

I lacked the necessary resources to work on my writing! I had a notebook with a broken screen, and a scrap for a smartphone with a dead battery! It was me, a single quire and a paper at hand every day, but the situation limited me in some way. It made it hard for me to write and edit my work as much as wanted to! It denied me flexibility in my writing!

The situation was tough that it even grew hard for me to write! The inspiration to write even abandoned me. I wrote less and less with each passing day! The pressure strangled me to the extent that, in attempt to remedy my financial struggle, I came close to an inch to selling one of my 'Pedi' poetry manuscripts! But, it just did not feel right at heart, so I withdrew from the idea!

I needed money to have decent clothes to wear my body! I needed money to be able to fix my notebook and my phone, or get new ones so that I could be able to write. To publish my work I needed money too! My life just did not flow because of being broke!

My situation pinned me down to a point of embarrassment and shame. Having no decent clothes to wear made it hard for me to walk the streets without thinking what other people thought of me. You get what I mean?

I mean, the people who are likely to make laughs of the next person's situation, are those we grew amongst and before their eyes. They are the people closest to us, people who know our struggles. They are those who have witnessed us try to climb the ladder to success, but kept falling. As much as a few will sympathize, many are likely to derive pleasure out of our unfortunate situations. People did derive laughs from unfortunate situation. I am a living testimony to that.

Some people had the guts to tell me I am nothing, *nothing but a dropout* in the presence of other people, just to make laughs about it! Some people derived laughs from my situation of lack. They made fun of me for wearing the same clothes every now and then! Some people tried to use me. They wanted to get their hands onto and to snatch away my hard written work, just because they thought I had no options!

I tried to reach out to people. Some of them sympathized whilst some gave me a sharp elbow to my heart, turned and looked the other way! From some I received promises on top of promises, expectations and dejections with them pulling out on me at the last second!

But, as much as I wanted to hate people for not wanting to help me, I chose otherwise. I had paused to read the picture with a sober mind and understanding to best interpret it. I understood purely that, people have intentions with their money. People cannot just go out of their way to give their hard earned money to the next person with ease, let alone a twenty seven years old man! *'No, it does not work that way'*, which is what I thought.

But, I knew deep inside, that I would never deprive anyone help if they were in need and I was able to help. I have always been generous my whole life besides not having. But, I just had to understand, that no two people are the same. I was me and the next person were them self, and had their own way of looking at things.

I was in need of a savior, but do not get me wrong, I was not looking for any favors. I related well with **Khalid** in his lyrics in the song *'Silence'* featured by **Marshmallow**. But, I had no one to turn to. Sometimes I just felt like waking up early in the morning, just pack my backpack with the few pity clothes I had, and just leave home even if I had nowhere to go. I would walk and keep on walking. *'It would be a whole lot better than being in a place where there was nothing for me'* I had thought.

But, some experiences in life, just break to mold us! My financial struggle did so with me! It was of lack that I had grown wiser and disciplined! It was of lack that had learned humility and to stay humbled at all times!

I had learned that, it is during the toughest times in one's life that people who care and those who do not give a damn get to stand out and show! It is when we are down, that the true colors of those in our life reveal them self! Those who care reach back and out, whilst those who do not just turn a blind eye, walk the other away and even make fun of one's unfortunate situations!

Living in lack has taught me that, money is a very important aspect of this life; that financial stability and freedom is crucial for a beautiful life; and that money is power! Black of white, believe it or not, money will always stand between us and our needs and wants!

'Money is the root of all evil' I hear some people say. *'But, from which perspective?'* I had paused and wondered to myself. I had come to believe otherwise myself, when the lack of money had stood before me, my needs and my dream; when I had had nowhere to go, when I had no decent clothes to wear, no food to feed my hunger, and all other sorts of essentials!

How could money be the root of all evil? It is more like a riddle waiting to be cracked! Money is only a commodity, an object. *The root of evil is in our thought; it is in the ideas we have about the means we want to use to get or to make use of the money!*

I had thought to myself 'the person who had passed this claim at first, must had had no money and, said this just to make them self feel better about not having money and to go on and suffer peacefully; or maybe they must had had money, a lot of it and used it for their evil deeds; or they must have witnessed people do evil deeds just to get money; or they must had been wise that, they realized that money can be the root of evil from either side of the coin! But, the fact remains, the root of evil is in our thought and ideas about how we want to attain or use money!

I once heard that: *'One's gift is what gives them a place in this world'* In trying to remedy my financial problem, and be able to turn my life around, I had decided to use the precious gift I have inside of me, the gift in writing! So I decided to give myself the task and challenge to write this beautiful book!

I had no idea where I was going to get the funds to self-publish the book though! There was no miracle that was going to happen for me to get the money to publish my book! There was no '*manna*' that was going to descend from any heaven! So I had to come up with plan!

I decided to put the idea of not having any funds to publish my book aside, and just focus on writing this book. It had been me, pen and paper, keyboard and a desktop screen, late night and in the early hours of the morning writing! The dawn greeted me and I waved bye to the setting sun! Day in and out, I was at it with my book!

Tough as it was, I had stood firm, focused and determined! I had the belief deep inside my core that, this book would be an amazing book, a good read and an important resource for self-help to the next person, and most importantly, the foundation to my career in writing! So, *I wrote, and I wrote and I wrote!*

In writing this book, I have prayed, meditated, did breathing exercises, affirmed, did yoga practice, to stay grounded, patient and focused! Something I did throughout all the other matters I will be discussing in the following couple of chapters.

But, as much as it was a hard task to complete this book, it was a fun and a very helpful toil! Writing this book presented me with the opportunity to look inwards and realize once more my true self, what I was about and what I wanted out of this life! It had also helped in raising my confidence and hopes of a better tomorrow!

With this chapter I aim to teach the next person that, money is the key to economic freedom! Money gives us options! Money can help us reach our dreams! Money can be a staircase and a stepping stone to our dreams! Money can help one mold their life towards the better!

The lack of it is just yet another obstacle which would most definitely deprive us the path towards meeting our needs and wants, reaching our dreams, molding and realizing a beautiful life!

Affirmation:

'I pour my soul into writing this book! I am inspired to write this book! It is an important book! I will write it passionately and patiently! I will finish, self-publish and sell it myself and change my life! And one day soon all will be well!'

Prayer:

'I pray to my spiritual guides to be with me, to protect, to give me the power and to guide me throughout my journey in writing this special book. I pray that I stay patient and write it from heart and not rush it. Amen!'

CHAPTER 6

The Anchor of the Past

Our encounters have an enormous impact upon our thought, our thought over our encounters have an enormous impact in the way we see and understand life, and how we see and understand life, has an immense impact in the way we behave, and the way we behave has a titanic impact in molding or tearing our life!

Once upon a not so beautiful life, I held on to the past. I dwelt upon the thoughts about what I had been put and gone through in my life in the past. I wondered how could and should my life had unfolded given I had not been put and gone through all the things I had been put and gone through as a kid!

I used to be angry---was angry for a very long time! I was angry of what other people have put me through in my life. I was angry with my parents for putting me in a place where my upbringing and childhood was unappealing and painful! I was angry with other people for their abuse and ill-treatment towards me as little kid! I felt a great deal of injustice inside of me my whole life!

I used to be angry with myself for dropping out of school; for losing out on such a crucial opportunity to obtain a degree! I used to wonder to myself, how my life could have unfolded if I had hung in there besides the depression and gotten my degree?

But, taking jaunts into the past and dwelling on the thoughts of what had gone down in the past, and getting worked up about it interfered with my calm and focus, and caused me unnecessary unrest and pain. This was not good for my health, both mentally and spiritually, and upon my overall life. It blinded me from seeing things clear, and disturbed my life's flow!

Getting worked up and angry towards the next person, for the things they had done to me, and being angry at myself for my past indecisions, decisions and mistakes, did me and my life no good at all! It was entirely unhealthy for my life! So, I had to deal with my past if I was to see progress with my life!

The Three Spaces of Time

The three spaces of time, being the past, the now and the future are a matter of yesterday, today and tomorrow; of what took, is taking and to take place; happened, happening and to happen; gone, going and to go; done, doing and to do; been, being and to be!

The Past

'*Show me a person who can unblink a blink, and I will unlaugh my laugh*'. I'm deeply sorry for breaking English just there. But, who could undo the past? The past is a fixed matter. In the past life has happened and nothing can be done with it. Everything is fixed. Period!

The Now

The now is a very special space of time. Life takes place, or rather I should say is taking place in '*the now*'. In the now we are awake and conscious of life. We have the power to do anything with our life, to build or tear.

This is where our focus should be paid. Because, the now is the only space of time we will ever exist within during this life. We can never exist in the past or in the future. The now is forever here and forever falling away into the fixed past!

The Future

The future has not happened. It is a forever arriving matter which gradually and with every second converts into 'the now'. We do not have to go wondering in the future. As much as we may have the confidence, we have to bear at mind the crucial fact that tomorrow is not promised for anyone, tomorrow is uncertain!

No one knows if they would still be here in the next tick of the clock. Life is not forever as time. We are not immortal. So we cannot go wasting our thought wondering in the future unknown. All that we have to do is to be tuned and focused in the now, because it is in *'the now'* that we are awake and are consciously witnessing life, no wonders and no imagination!

Dropping the Anchor of the Past

Forgiving and Letting Go

I once heard that, **'forgiveness is an act of self-relief'**, and the starting point of letting go and healing! So, in trying to deal with my ugly past, I decided to forgive myself and those who have done me wrong. I decided to learn from my past instead. I chose to forgive!

I had to make peace with my bad past; do away with the anger and hate that had long brewed inside of me. I had to stop pointing fingers, casting blame or seeking revenge. It did me no good, not even a bit! It had interfered with my focus. It had delayed my progress in life. And, I just could not afford any more setbacks in my life any longer.

I needed to focus to get to my dreams. I could not afford nor allow anything to disturb that. It was time I dealt with my past and made peace with it. No matter how tough! No matter what! It was time I buried the past forever!

Besides, there is nothing one can do to change the past. It's something which is fixed, something we have no power over. Worrying about an ugly past causes us unnecessary pain and setbacks. It benefits us not, not in any way. It delays progress and, cripples our dreams!

So, I had decided to forgive myself. And, at a great deal of expense, I had decided to let go of my relationship with some of the other people who brought pain into my life and continued to do so!

I had decided to forgive myself for dropping out of varsity because; I had realized that I had a bigger aim and that was to fight tooth and nail with depression! The matter had been that, when things did not work out the way I wanted with my life, I got scared, impatient and got blinded of my crucial objectives. I found myself lingering in the past, fiddling for faults and beating myself up for them!

I had taken the decision to accept that I could not change the past! If there was anything that I could do about the past it was to let it go, *'let go, to get going'*. I had to let the past be, focus in and do my best in the now, and work towards a better tomorrow! In the process of letting go of my past and making peace with it, I began to heal, both mentally and emotionally! And, I focused more on my life in the now other than the past!

I had learned that, although other people have put me through what they had in the past, it did not mean that people with beautiful minds, beautiful hearts; people that are loving and caring; people who meant well by me did not exist anymore. It had not been fair of me to rule out everyone else in the world because of a few people who had hurt me.

I had paused at this important point in my life; looked around me, and realized that, I had been blinded by hurt and anger, to see things clear! I had the most amazing people around me, people who have always stood by me and shown me love!

I had people who have always been a beautiful part of my life; people who truly loved and appreciated and meant well by me. I always had loving friends who stood by me through black and white. I have always had shelter in the love of a true friend and comfort in their support!

I had come to learn that **blood ties means nothing as long as there is no love**! A stranger/s can be the family we never had. A stranger can show the next person love, care, empathy, respect and appreciation than those we are tied to by blood!

In accepting, forgiving and letting go, I had dealt away with 'the anchor of the past'. I had gotten rid of an unnecessary burden over my life. Now I could focus on fixing my life without bothering about what could have or should had been with my life!

I had learned that, harmony and justice is written in our thought and dreams! And, **the best revenge we are ever going to get is written in our success**! So, why not let go of the past and let our mind be occupied with beautiful thoughts and the ideas about our dreams?

I used to look at my past and shed tears. The thought that I could have ended my life back then, and that I would not be here right now, hurts me deep down! I am so lucky and, it is by chance that I am still here! I am grateful to be here! I am grateful that I am still alive!

I no longer look at my previous encounters, from the ill-treatment in my childhood, to the depression I had and my mistakes and cry! No! I am only grateful that I went through it all! Because **I had come out of the cocoon of it all a better self, wise and strong**!

I now look at my distant past and I say these words: "*Encounters and experiences are what build a person towards a greater character*'. If it was possible for me to go back into the past and change anything about it, I would not dare, for I appreciate how my life had unfolded, or else I would not be the person I am today!

Though it was a painful and sorrowful past, from it I had learned a lot! You know what they say, '*experience is the best teacher?*' My tough upbringing made me grow wiser. It had molded me into a stronger and a special person!

We do not have any power over the past! The only power we have is to learn from it. Good or bad, **the past can be a good teacher**. From it we can draw lessons, accumulate wisdom and inspiration which might prove crucial down the road!

The past is not ours to change, or the future. All that we can do is decide in 'the now', whether we keep holding on to the past and let it mess up our calm and focus in the now, or we let go and invest our time and thought upon beautiful deeds, beautiful deeds which would bring light to the picture of the past, make us enjoy life in the now, and conquer the unknown future? **If we do beautiful things right now, the past cannot judge us harshly, and the future is already defeated**!

We cannot keep lingering and holding on to the past. Dwelling on the misfortunes or our past mistakes is only damaging. It causes unnecessary pain upon our lives. At some point we have got to drop the anchor of, bury and let go of the past! We got to make peace with the past, invest our precious thought on beautiful ideas, focus in the now and move on with life!

Affirmation:

'I know I had gone through a lot in the past. But I cannot do anything to change it. I accept my past for what it is. I forgive those who had wronged me. I forgive myself for my past mistakes. And I let go of the past. I focus in the now.'

Prayer:

'To my spiritual guides, I pray for the strength to forgive and let go of the past and focus in the now. Amen!'

CHAPTER 7

The Ring of Terror

'*It had been a foolish and an act of self-betrayal, and life proved painful for the lavender which wanted to be like the sunflower!*' One grandmother once said to her beloved little granddaughter who was too caught up in the idea of making her skin complexion brighter, just because she wanted to be like her friend who had a natural lighter skin complexion!

This births wonder! If we took a closer and a careful look at it, we would realize it truly raises wonder! I mean, should a horse or a donkey have a problem about not having the black and white stripes like the zebra? What about the hedgehog and the porcupine? What about the lion and the tiger? Get the picture?

Once upon a not so beautiful life, when things did not work out with my life, I compared myself with other people. I took a look around and saw that my friends and peers had better lives compared to that of mine.

Most of my friends and peers appeared to have their lives all figured out. They had gotten their degrees, gotten good paying jobs, living in their own homes, in their own houses, driving their own cars! Some of them even gotten married, had children, and had their own families.

I paused and thought to myself '*What about me?*' Well, nothing worked out with my life yet. My life had been a merry-go-round---

a spiraling matter! It was filled up with U-turns and detours over the years! I had not gotten anywhere or any far with my life!

The comparison I made landed me in the cruelest place, a place which I refer to as '*the ring of terror!*' It was a place I built myself, my own creation, in my own mind and with my own thought!

Within this so called 'ring of terror', I had a terrific and the most terrifying battle, with my own thoughts, thoughts which came from the comparison I passed between myself, my friends and peers!

I felt great shame with myself, because most of my peers and friends appeared to be 'up there', whilst I appeared to be down on the ground, shipwrecked! This messed up my self-esteem and confidence big time! I felt enormously reduced and so small!

The comparison made me feel like a complete failure and a loser! I felt as though I got chewed up by life, spit out, and all that was left of me was only a mere worthless frame walking the earth's premises!

The situation caused me to go peeping into the past. It made me wonder what my life could have been and how it could have unfolded if I had finished my studies and procured my degree in B.com Economics! Something I had mentioned in the previous chapter.

With each and every jaunt I made into the past, I returned with nothing but pain in the now! This resulted from the constant wonder about what I could have, should have done, how I could have handled things and how things could have turned out if I had completed and gotten my degree! It all left me with a plentiful of 'maybes' and a sack full of regrets!

'Maybe if I had gotten my degree, I would be somewhere up there; I would have a job myself, my own car, my own house and family; I would not be down here feeling guilty, feeling a failure, a loser, and a disappointment to myself and to other people'.

The comparison made me want to prove a point to other people. I felt the need to prove other people wrong, especially the people who laughed at my unfortunate situation, when I had been struggling and things just did not work out with my life, yet!

I so wanted to prove a point to people who made laughs of me when I had lived in lack; when I had worn torn up clothes; the people who tried to take advantage of me because of my situation and wanted to use me!

But, deep in the cores of my heart, to want to prove a point to the next person just did not feel right; because, down this road, the *bristly* road of comparison, I lost my true identity! **I forgot who I truly was, was about and what life really meant to me**! I forgot what I love, what I am passionate of and what my dreams were!

Comparing myself with others derailed me from my own rail towards my dreams and from my own rail of life! I found myself striding the wrong path! I got lost in trying to prove a point to the world! I got too caught up in trying to be like other people instead of being my true self!

I got caught up in trying to climb the wrong ladder in life just to appear equivalent to, or to surpass the standards of those I had compared myself with! I wanted to live my life on a level measured upon the comparison I made between myself and other people, just to appear cool to the world!

See, the Comparison we make of our self with the next person and getting worked up emotionally about it all, *is a pure act of self-betrayal!* Imagine wasting a second, a minute, a day, weeks, months, years, our precious life time wanting to live our lives in ways which are not what we personally want, just because we want to prove a point to the next person; to appear cool to the world! Wouldn't it be a long painful and a wasted life time at our ultimate end?

Some things in life are painted to us in black and white, not cryptic and not complex, but for us to grasp with ease. But, *'do we get the picture?'* Do not we go on to suffer because of our lack of thought, misinterpretations, and lack of understanding and bad choices? Which then turns and makes us fall victims of our own making?

We were born alone! Were we not? Our life's journey is our own! Is it not? Who we truly are, is in our natural identity! It is written in our birthright and our dreams! We just have to keep reminding ourselves who we are and why we are here! Who we are is something which is within us, something which cannot be determined by others. Should not we embrace who we truly are?

It is rather unfair for one to compare themself with others; because, we and the next person are not the same. If we took a careful look we would realize that our encounters and experiences in life are not the same as those of the next person, whom we compare our self with!

We may find that we have been through worse, or they had been through far worse than us themselves, or what they had been through is nothing compared to what we had been through in our own life! Our life's journey is not the same as that of the next person nor does it turn out the same!

No one knows the self better than self itself! Every person in the world has their own idea of what success means to them. Success is something which is in line with our innermost honest dreams! But, if we went on to live our lives in comparison of the self with other people, we risk losing our true identity in the process. I did myself; lose the sense of my true self; strode the road which was never mine nor meant for me to begin with; and I arrived nowhere but in the destination filled with uncertainty and dissatisfaction!

I had to look into the mirror of truth. I peeped into the lake of my soul and asked myself these questions: *'Who am I? What is life for me? What is my dream? What is my purpose here?'* I had to find myself. I had to remind myself who I was, was about, what life meant to me and what my dreams were. I did!

Constructive Comparison

Comparing one's self with the next person is not a bad thing all to all! I see you wearing a cloth of wonder upon your face and wondering, *'how is that possible?'* Well in truth, self-comparison is not bad all to all; because something good can come out of the comparison we make if we chose to believe otherwise. The comparison we make of the self with others can be a helpful factor in improving our self and one's life!

There is a pure difference between us comparing the self and getting jealous and sad and wanting to be like or to surpass the next person we are comparing the self with, and comparing the self with the very same person and drawing inspiration to improve!

There is an enormous difference between the person who tells us: *'learn from your friend'* and the person who tells us: *'Your friends had gotten far with this life and you're still in the ground!'*

Instead of comparing ourselves with others and letting the result bring us down emotionally, we could learn to draw inspiration from the next person; inspiration to work towards achieving our own dreams instead of being in pursuit of success measured in comparison to that of the next person!

Yes, when things have not worked out in one's life yet; when we are still at it and take a look around and find that our peers and friends have flourished in their lives; when people are laughing at and comparing us to others themselves; we might find that we want to make comparison of our own selves to the next person, and end up envying, wanting to be like or better than those we are compared to!

But in the face of all that, we should and must remember who we are and are about! I repeat *'Nobody knows the self better than the self itself!'* We should remember our dreams. Our dreams are what define our life's journey and give it meaning!

At the end of the day, the life worth living is one upon which we live as the true self; working towards achieving and living out the dreams inside of us! Because to try to surpass the next person, to try to appear cool to the world, or to try to please the next person might have us living out the life which is not our own, but to end up wafting through this life!

I worked hard to break away from the comparison I made of myself with my friends, peers or any other person; and I managed to jump outside the 'ring of terror'. My self-focus and the focus upon my own life's journey and dreams appeared purer and vivid!

Affirmation:

'I am Samuel! I love and I am passionate with writing. I do not just write, I write from heart; to provoke thought; to impart wisdom; to touch the lives of others and inspire a beautiful life! That's my purpose in this world!'

Prayer:

'To you my spiritual guides; I pray for the strength to accept my current situation in my life; to not go comparing and wanting be like or to be better than other people, but be my own true self! Amen!'

CHAPTER 8

The not so Beautiful People

'No man is an island' the saying goes. It makes no wonder that since our birth, we always had people in our lives; and that as we walked this earth, we met with and continued to build relationships with other people. It is all natural for a person to, and that a person has got to have people to walk with upon their life's journey!

But, the presence of other people; what one thinks and feels of them; and the behavior of the particular people around them, will always touch and influence one's life, in a good or in a bad way! The people one chooses to share their life's journey with, will either be a beautiful part of and add value to, or be an unappealing part and cause disruption upon one's life!

It is very crucial for one to have the sort of people who are, would be and remain a beautiful part of, and impact their life in a good way! One should not have in their life, the sort people who are an ugly part of and bring destruction and pain upon their life!

People are meant to come together for a very good course in this life. People are meant to cooperate, help one another grow and share a beautiful life! So, a person has got to be careful who they tag along with, bring into and share their life's journey with!

I used to have people in my own life whose mere presence and toxic behaviors just touched my life in a very unappealing way!

Around these people I would feel a great deal of discomfort and a stir up in my emotions! Their presence would just paint my mood dull!

Some of the people were those that have caused me pain my whole life. The sort of people I kept in my life and shared spaces with because they and I were tied by DNA or deeply cared for! But, their presence caressed my life bitterly!

I had friends with toxic behaviors whom I continued to hang around with regardless of their behaviors. But, I suffered unrest due to that! Far worse, I witnessed myself succumb to and adopt their behaviors, which in turn just did not work well for me!

With this I learned that, we tend to suffer sometimes, because we love too much, we are too attached or we feel obliged to hold on to certain people in our lives! We continue holding on to the relationships we have with others no matter how bad it impacts our wellbeing, which is unhealthy!

Maybe we are blinded by the love we have for the next person. Maybe we remain hopeful they would change for the better even if they do not! Maybe we are too attached to let go. Maybe we keep leaning on them because we feel like we cannot make it without them. Maybe we just want to keep appearing cool to and keep pleasing the world. Well, who knows?

But is it worth it? Is it worth the interference in our peace of mind? Does it worth the stir up in our emotions and the unrest at heart? I bet it is not, not even a tiny bit! Every person wants peace of mind and calm in their life!

If we are ever to maintain peace of mind and rest at heart; if we are ever to maintain calm and focus, and make sound decisions in life, we have to do away with toxic people! We have to walk away or make them walk; especially if they are not willing to make an effort to change and become better people and a beautiful part of our lives.

As much as it may sound harsh and a bitter pill to swallow, one cannot afford to waste their thought on people who do not add value to their life but bring only disruption! There is neither excuse, nor a room for debate on this one! It is a neutral, pure and uncontested truth!

We have to draw the lines and make sure that, the people we hang around with and anyone who wants to be part of our life, are beautiful souls; the sort of people who would make an effort to be a beautiful part of our lives!

Harsh as it may sound to the next person, it does not matter who the toxic person may be, as long as they are not making an effort to be better people and be a beautiful part of and keep causing harm to one's life, they just do not deserve to be a part of it!

We are people 'walking' in a very cruel world; trying to figure out what life is about in a tough age and time; trying to figure out our lives. We are people trying to get to their dreams! All this needs a sober mind. With all that is going on in the world and the lot we take intake into our minds every day, one cannot afford to pay a toxic person no mind!

Every person has the freedom to choose who they want to be part of and who they want to tag along in their life's journey! It is one's own decision and not anyone else's. It is a decision and a choice which rests entirely upon one's own hands!

In my road towards building a healthy peaceful life, I had recognized the need to do away with certain people in my life. Either I walked or I made them walk! I vowed to myself that, anyone who wanted to be a part of my life, would have to be a beautiful soul!

They must have a beautiful mind and heart, behaviors and attitudes, care about and respect other people! No exceptions, no excuses! I wanted people with beautiful minds and hearts, behaviors and attitudes; people who cared, respected and meant well by me; people who are passionate in having and living out a beautiful life them self; people with whom I would cooperate and collaborate with in harmony and help one another grow in and journey harmoniously through this life!

Our relationships, in our life's journey ought to be beautiful ones; they are ought to be made out of people who mean well; the sort of people who add value into our life; the sort of people who love, respect and care about us; people who inspire and help us grow; people with beautiful minds and hearts, behaviors and attitudes; people we would cooperate with and share our life's journey with in harmony!

Who are those sorts, if not beautiful people?

Affirmation:

'I have always made an effort to remain a beautiful part of other people's lives. So, I am not wrong to not want toxic people in my life! I deserve to and I choose to share my life with beautiful people'.

Prayer:

'To you my spiritual guides I pray for the strength to be and remain a beautiful part of other people's lives! May those who are not willing to make an effort to be a beautiful part of my life stand it afar! Amen!'

CHAPTER 9

Fear

Fear! Every person has their own fears! We all have the fear for something. We fear the known and the unknown, the visible and the invisible, the true and the untrue, the possible and the impossible and, our fears can be reasonable and understandable or unreasonable and absurd!

Some people are fearful towards deities, hell or aliens; some people have the fear for disease, curse and death; some have the fear for heights or the darkness; some have the fear for certain creatures; and some people are fearful of harm, heartbreak and sadness.

But, most of us seem to allow our fears to curb us from meeting our aims with life. We allow our fears to take the position of captaincy; to give commands; and to stand behind the steering wheel and control our lives, without even realizing the fact! For example: the fear of failure; fear of disappointment or, the fear of being ridiculed! Such fears blind us and hold us back and delay progress with our lives.

We keep at it even though we recognize the damage it does upon our lives. Why? Why does this occur? Well, it occurs because we have granted fear power over our lives in the first place!

We have learned to listen to the whispers of pessimism from our fears; which kills our confidence and courage; our enthusiasm and inspiration in working towards realizing our lives' most important aims. Which is just not the good way to go by with this life?

I used to be fearful myself! I used to be fearful of things turning out wrong for me; fearful of failure; and fearful of being ridiculed! Further worse, I used to be fearful of success; fearful of ascending over to my life stage; fearful of being looked upon by others; fearful of blundering or being scorned for my achievements!

Fear told me: '*What if? What if it does not work out? What if you get humiliated or get ridiculed for your work?*' I listened to the whispers of my fears and took shelter in hiding, in the *comfort zone*, away from the risk of things going wrong; away from failure, disappointment, ridicule and humiliation!

But, it did not feel right at heart, not even a tiny bit! Because, I so wanted to play the protagonist in my life's story! But, I allowed fear to stand in my way! I wanted to write my life's story, a special and a beautiful story, but I had let fear hold the pen, to spill the ink and write an unappealing tale!

I so wanted to paint a beautiful picture out of my life, but I had let fear hold on to the painting brush. I had let fear paint a picture not appealing at all out of my life. This made my life all dull and gloomy!

I so wanted to ascend over to my life stage; to climb the staircase to success, but I had let fear pull me down! I was fearful of the spotlight; what the reactions of other people might be; fearful of being ridiculed or being laughed at by other people!

See, fear can, to some extent, a greater extent, be a person's greatest hurdle and weakness! It can cause one to lose confidence in them self and upon their dreams. It can kill our drive towards achievement! It can cripple or make us walk away from our dreams; cause us to paint a dull picture out of our life; and most importantly, cause us to lose out on our precious time!

But, should we allow our fears to stand between us and our life's most crucial goals; to pull us back and hold us down? Should we allow our fears to come between us and our dreams; to delay and cause us to walk away from our dreams? 'No!' I hear you say.

But what should we do in the face of our fears? We can choose to be brave! Bravery is our strongest weapon in dealing with our fears! Bravery is our wings, ones which can carry us over the barriers of our fears! Because, bravery can help us summon self-confidence; and self-confidence can help us break barriers!

I have learned myself, the hard way of course, after losing out on so many precious opportunities and after losing out on my precious time revolving in circles because of fear that, black or white, like it or not, *one has to face and deal with their fears a whole lot sooner!* It is something that has to be done; something which has to happen eventually if we are to make progress with our lives and realize our dreams! Because if not, we risk our dreams being delayed; fading away; not making any progress with our life; losing out on time; and living a life full of regrets about what and how life could have turn out if we had not allowed fear to hold control over our life! Success will seem to grow further and further away from our reach. And our life will be one filled with regrets and pain!

See, I love writing! I am very passionate with writing! I do it out of heart! I have deep respect for the art! It has always been my dream to become one of the greatest authors in the world! To carve words with love and passion, and to share beautiful ideas and stories, and to provoke thought, touch a heart and the lives of other people with this divine art!

In writing I find myself! I find purpose and meaning; pleasure and delight! If I am not a writer who am I? What am I here for, what's my purpose here? If my work is not out there and not being read by the world, what am I writing for?

Why aren't I a published author? Why isn't my work out there yet? Because of what, fear? How long shall I allow fear to hold me back from realizing my dream? Is fear this powerful over my life that I will let it kill my dream?

'*No! Something has to be done about this; I certainly have to do something!*' I told myself. I had a dream to achieve, the dream of becoming a published author! I had a dream of having a beautiful life. Writing formed a great part of that dream. I refused to be the victim of fear; refused fear to have control over my life!

See, there is a vast difference between a man who runs away in sight of a sleeping lion in the wild; a man who takes cautious action to make a safe pass; and the man who stands in bravery to fight the same lion if it had attacked!

'*Moa mahlong a tau o ya a swere serumula*' a 'Pedi' man once said. This is a wise 'Pedi proverb' which interprets: '*A person goes before the lion's face with a burning torch in their hand*'. This proverb explained means that, one goes into the battle prepared, knowing what they are up against. This symbolizes an act of bravery!

See, I had lacked bravery myself in letting my fears control my life in the past. In fearing things turning out wrong, being ridiculed, successful and being looked up at by others. But as much as I dwelt my thought upon the idea I realized that I was fearful of a sleeping and a harmless lion!

I never really tried to work a way around my fears. All I did was to run away! But, it was about time, after living on the ground because of my fears, to work my way around them; to hold the burning torch in my hand, walk passed the sleeping lion and look it in the eye if it had woken!

So, I told myself that, from now onwards, I am brave, the bravest man alive! I had decided to face my fears; to stare fear in the eye and say: '*I run the show in my life now, not you!*' I decided to take control, to take risks, risks of ascending over to my life stage. I realized this was something I should have done a long, *very* long time ago!

I vowed to myself that, **I will be fearful of fear itself!** I will be fearful of wasting my precious time here, in this world! I will fear wasting my precious once off gift (My life). I will be fearful of wafting through this life; fearful of dying not having reached and lived my dreams; fearful of dying just Sam; and fearful of dying without having truly lived this life!

Our fears do not have that much power over us, unless we allow it to be so! We are powerful than our fears would appear to be. We just have to believe that we are greater than our fears! Because we are truly greater than our fears may appear to be!

In learning to deal with my fears, to stare them in the eyes, I gave myself the challenge to write, finish and publish this book! Something I had mentioned previously. I told myself that '*no matter what the odds may be I will write, finish and publish this book!*' I decided that it was time I became the author I had always dreamt of becoming. I would not allow anything to stand in my way, not fear and or any other obstacle, never!

Constructive Fear

And I hear you say: '*Could fear really be useful?*' Oh yes it can!

Let us take a man who fears evil, truly and honestly fears evil for a clear example of the idea of constructive fear. What would the character of such a man be? Would not their fear over evil make them a very special person? I mean, if they feared evil, would not it mean that, they wanted nothing to do with evil at all? Would it not mean that they went against all sorts of evil, that they refrained from evil them self?

Would not their self conduct be one of a kind? I mean, if they feared evil they walked away from evil; would do anything in their power to fight and overcome all sorts of evil, which meant that, they meant well for them self and towards others. Would not their intentions and behaviors be, if not the squeakiest, pure; which in turn meant that their fear over evil had a beautiful impact upon their life? Get the idea?

The fear of fear itself: If we feared fear itself it means that we just do not fear at all. Fear does not have any power over our life in any way! This is good being that, it helps us to detect and to counter the thoughts of fear before they could even influence our life. It helps us to gather courage, and to stand with confidence against any opponent, be it fear or any other obstacle we met with in life.

The fear of running out of time: *'Time waits for no man'* a wise man once said. We are not immortal. Our life is not eternal! We are not going to be here for long! Sooner or later our life is going to reach an end!

But, even so, we should not fear death! We should fear dying without having lived out our dreams or having not tried! This idea in itself is the source of motivation for us to refrain from wasting our limited precious time in this world on worthless things!

This motivates us to invest and use our time over important matters. It motivates us to live an important life, a life full of purpose and meaning! And, would not a life full of purpose and meaning be one which is beautiful?

After all, a beautiful life is what we had come into this world to live. So, our fear of running out of time will help us work towards achieving our important life's aims and realizing a beautiful life at the end! And somewhere between our birth and death have and live a beautiful life!

The fear of losing out on opportunities: Success is the accumulation of our small aims. If we are to realize a beautiful life, we should be fearful of losing out and begin to grasp each and every opportunity presented to us where possible! Because, the very opportunities, if seized and used will form part of our success, which will help us realize our dreams, and in realizing our dreams we will definitely realize a beautiful life!

See, it is when and until we had decided to face and deal with our fears; when we had stopped fearing the unseen, the impossible, the absurd; when we had stopped composing horrible movies directed by fear in our minds; when we decide to counter our fears with bravery; and face our truest and realest fears that; we begin to witness and seize every opportunity presented to us along our life's journey that; we realize progress in our life and begin pursuing and reaching our dreams! And by so doing, we get closer and closer towards realizing a beautiful life!

Affirmation:
'I am brave. I am no longer scared! I am bigger than my fears! I do not give a damn any longer what the reactions of others may be. I am doing me! That's all that matters!'

Prayer:
'To you my spiritual guides I pray that you give me the strength to remain brave throughout my life's journey. I ask for the strength to

remain brave and calm in the face of any damaging reactions by people!'

CHAPTER 10

The Awakening

'*What is this that is happening to me? What is this I am experiencing? What is this beautiful feeling I am having? Where is it all coming from?*' I wondered to myself, wondered to myself in the midst of an awakening, my spiritual awakening!

The experience was so divine and miraculous! It was astonishing and marvelous; surprising and wondrous; so amazing and so precious! The feeling it brought to my heart was the most beautiful feeling I had never felt my whole life!

For the very first time in my life, I felt completely reborn and rejuvenated mentally, physically and spiritually! I felt completely calm and focused; worry free; patient and passionate; uplifted and inspired; light and free; cheerful and happy; in tune and connected with all of life around me; felt alive, truly alive!

For the first time in my whole life, I paused patiently, took a patient, calm, focused and a passionate look at life! All that I could see, all that I witnessed with my eyes was miraculous and beautiful, beautiful beyond measure!

I perceived life through a rejuvenated and refined mind and sight! It felt as though I was asleep all my life, like I had just woken to this miraculous and a beautiful thing called life! I saw beauty with my physical and spiritual sight; interpreted it in my thought and felt it deep within the wells of my heart!

I observed beauty out of life through all my senses! What I saw with my eyes; all the beautiful patterns in all of nature, so vivid and so colorful; the feeling of all that I could touch; the feeling of water running upon my body; the feeling of the wind caressing my flesh; the taste and warm energy in the food I ate; all this filled my thought with wonder and caressed my heart with the most beautiful feeling ever!

I paused to admire the miraculous works of nature! I witnessed and admired the splendid art in all of nature's works! I saw beauty everywhere! I witnessed beauty in a flower and admired its beautiful patterns and fragrance! I saw beauty in a butterfly; in the way it flapped its wings and danced in the sky! I saw beauty in a tree and felt something when I touched its leaves!

I saw beauty in the dusk and the dawn, in the rising and the setting of the sun! I saw beauty in the patterns drawn by the clouds upon the skies! I paused, looked up and admired the beauty in the glittering objects decorating the night's skies, the stars!

I looked around and saw beautiful people in my fellow humans, fellow companions in the journey of life! I witnessed beauty in the face of a little kid! I admired the smile decorated upon a stranger's face! I felt happy inside to see other people joyful and happy!

For the first time in my life, I felt deeply inspired! I felt deeply confident with myself! I felt like I could do anything if I dared to! I felt like I could take on any challenge no matter how big it was! I felt like I could overcome anything that life threw at me! I grew patient! I felt love, and all that resonated from it! I felt compassionate, empathetic, and passionate and care towards all of life!

For the first time in my life, I woke up in the morning and felt positive and optimistic! I woke and I felt like telling those around me that I love them so much, which I did! I felt like standing at the peaks of the biggest mountain in the world and tell the whole world that '*Life is so beautiful!*'

'*So this is what it feels like to be alive, truly alive? If this is how it feels to be alive then, this is how life should and ought to be! No matter what, a person should strive to have this form of life! It is beautiful!*' I thought to myself.

In this divine and miraculous experience, I learned that, the meaning of life is something which is felt; that no matter how much the world tried to explain the meaning of life, the next person may wonder at the idea of a meaningful life without ever really realizing firsthand the meaning of life which can only be explained by the feeling of being truly alive!

CHAPTER 11

The Pupils of Our Encounters

As we walk this earth, living our life in this critical world where so much bad than good is happening, bad natural or unnatural is likely to touch our lives, whether we like it or not! We are bound to meet with encounters which will most definitely influence our lives in some way!

It is a critical world our world, with so much bad than good going on all around! We will if we are fortunate enough, bump across a bountiful of good encounters which will touch our lives in a beautiful way. Not because we are special in any way because even death does not discriminate amongst the mortals, but because things are just fortunately working in our favor!

But if not fortunate, we will meet with some bad encounters which will touch our lives in an ugly way, bring unbearable pain and cause life to be unpleasant! Not because we are bad in any way nor we did not deserve, but because we were just unfortunate!

How many people wanted to be abused during their childhood? How many people wanted to be the victims of domestic violence; victims of rape; and victims of mockery just because of particular situations with their life?

How many people wanted to be the victims of a dreadful accident; a natural disaster or war? How many people wanted to be victims of disease or any other condition and lay in a hospital bed? How many people who died unexpectedly or knowingly that their time had come wanted it to be so? Get the sense behind the idea?

We are just people living in a critical world where so much is happening as I have said; a whole lot which is natural, unnatural and orchestrated which our lives are exposed to, which can touch and influence our lives in some way, directly or indirectly!

Let us take an idea of a bad parent who abuses their child. The child is purely innocent! They not deserve such a bad treatment! They deserve to be shown great care and love. But in opposition to the love and care, the parent pulled a bad act towards them, which impacted the child in a bad way physically, socially, emotionally and psychologically!

If the child was to grow passed the abuse, should they live with the trauma they had suffered from the abuse brought unto them by a bad parent during their childhood? Should they adopt such a gesture and apply it in their parenthood? Should they go on to abuse their own children? Should they not learn from their previous encounter, out of primal wisdom, and show their kid/s or any other person love? Could they not make a better social worker or therapist tomorrow?

One other clear example would be a natural matter. For example, a tornado, which happened to befall the land which we are living in and caused severe damage; this would touch and influence our life to some extent!

Another clear example would be orchestrated matter! Let us look at a war outbreak in the nation we lived in. And assume that during that war, homes got destroyed and many people lost their precious lives but we fortunately survived the war.

Should we go on to live the rest of our lives in fear, anger, and blame, and in the lookout for revenge when all the war had passed? Should we orchestrate our own war to avenge ourselves? Should not we learn to resolve feuds between two parties with a conversation? Become the better leader who values the right of '*all of life*' to life?

The sense I am trying to make with all this is that, we are living this life in a world where anything from any direction can come and touch our life in some way! No matter what our encounters might be; no matter how much the pain it may bring upon our life; we should learn from our encounters!

Our world is like a mud pit of bad than good, we just have to learn how to wash away the dirt, and learn how cherish the good and continue forth with life! Because, most of the encounters we meet with along the road, come and hit our lives in the absence of expectation!

But, the encounters we meet with in our life's journey are not for us to quit and to go bailing out on this life! They are for us hard as they may be, to welcome, to meet with them with boldness, to go through them, to battle with; to learn and grow from and to conquer them!

Our encounters are the refining sources towards a better character and a better life! It is from our harshest encounters and from our experiences that we come out refined and stronger individuals than we could imagine!

It is from the harshest of encounters which life throws at us that, we learn the most important and crucial life lessons about life! The very lessons in turn help us to understand more and deal better with life's most critical and crucial matters!

See, education is not always about going to a place so called 'school', sitting behind the desk, studying a book or waiting for someone to stand before us and educate us, no! Education is everywhere! Education is in the behavior of all of life which surrounds us! Just, we have to pause sometimes so that we can be able to pick it all up and realize it!

The most important education regarding life is going to come from our personal encounters as we continue to walk this earth! It is from our encounters we learn. As long as we walk this earth we are in class like every day. We are bound to have encounters, of which we have to welcome with an open mind and learn from!

We are the pupils of our encounters! It is from our encounters, good and bad that we build experience; from our experience that we build wisdom; from our wisdom that we build a better character and from the better character that we build a better life! Without encounter, where is experience? Without experience where is wisdom? Without wisdom, where is understanding; where is the resolve? Without resolve where is realization and progression?

Yes, I had a painful upbringing; was a victim of abuse as a kid; and the victim of mockery. Yes, people made laughs of my dark skin complexion! Yes, people chased me away from their homes! Yes, people casted me out and made the little me feel like an outcast.

Yes, I had lived with depression. Yes, depression made my life a living hell for some time. Yes, depression pushed me to walk at the edges of my life every day. Yes, at a multiple of occasions I nearly took my own life.

Yes, fear pinned me down so hard, held me back and down and delayed my dreams. Yes, poverty oppressed my life. Yes, people walked out on me in the times of need. Yes, I had lived in lack; I had no penny written to my name; I had dressed in tatters and rags. Yes, people used me! Yes, people laughed at me.

Yes, I had compared myself with others! I had been envious! I wanted to appear better than the next person. I wanted to appear cool to the world. I wanted to please other people. And I have lost my true self along the way.

Yes, I had held on to the past. I was angry! I had held on to grudges! I casted blame unto others my whole life! I always felt a great deal of injustice. I used to be in the lookout for revenge. I lost faith in people! Yes, I had let toxic people influence my life with their toxic behaviors for some time! I had let people who brought me and continued to bring me pain to stay in my life!

But, something beautiful came out of it all. I came out of it all strong! All the encounters I had gone through, although painful and hard to bear with, helped me grow! They made me consult life's most basic but crucial matters. They shoved me to make critical but crucial adjustments in regard with my life! And I had grown a little bit wiser!

I have learned to value and respect what is important. I have learned to value this chance I was given at this thing called life; to appreciate and respect this once off precious gift! I have learned that I have the right to a beautiful life! I have learned to take care for myself mentally, physically and spiritually.

I have learned to show myself the love those around me have failed to show me my whole life; love so honest and so true! I learned to not expect the next person to tell me that they love me. I fell in true love with my true self! And now I understood firsthand what **Akua Naru** really meant when she said '*Self-love is the very first romance!*'

Should I have known better; should I have had the wisdom, maybe I could have handled all the matters with my life differently. But to know better is to have knowledge. And, the knowledge we have is the source of our wisdom! So I had to learn and gather knowledge along the way.

You may have been abused in anyway like I have been in the past! You may have been made to feel like an outcast and a reject or feeling so right now; you may be feeling like you do not belong.

You may be feeling all alone; feeling like nobody cares. You may be a laughing stock to the people around you because of some unfortunate conditions with your life; just, *do not go giving up* on your life!

You may be going through a painful challenge right now! You may be stuck at the crossroads right now; confused, stressed out, fearful, depressed and panicking! You may be facing the steepest uphill to climb and to ascend over! The road may be full of thorns! It may be hurting so badly where you are in your life right now! You may be feeling like you do not deserve to be in this world; like you do not deserve to be alive; *just do not go giving up on your life!*

Because, one day soon, all the wounds and the pain resulting from our hardships and trials in life do heal! All the pain disappears into the distant past and become only memories! We grow in all the crucial areas of life; our life begins to make sense; we learn to live our life in the most crucial way and finally our life blossoms and become beautiful!

We will realize that beyond all the painful encounters there is a very beautiful world, where a beautiful life awaits us! And, we will yet be grateful that we did not go pulling the plugs at that moment of pain and desperation, where we felt like we had no option and assumed death as our only way out!

Beyond the depression; beyond the negative thoughts; beyond our bad past; beyond our fears; beyond our financial struggles; beyond any bad habits; beyond the comparison of the self with other people; beyond the broken bridge towards our dreams; beyond any possible encounter we meet with along in our life's journey, there is something so precious which awaits us and that is A BEAUTIFUL LIFE!

References

Live Sonima(2016)Guided Meditation to Boost Energy with Deepak Chopra. Available at: https//youtu.be/Xk8AnUnKdsg (Accessed: 19 December 2020).

Prince Ea(2016)YOU ARE NOT DEPRESSED, STOP IT! . Available at: https//youtu.be/ykvC3QXJb18(Accessed: July 2017)

Akua Naru(2012)Akua Naru- This Mo(u)rning feat. Drea d'Nur //"Live & Aflame Sessions"(MTV TheWrapUp Premiere). Available at: https//youtu.be/h2ka2v9Z9Us(Accessed: 28nSeptember 2017

A Beautiful Life, a Dream!

Let it be!

Ke a leboga!

(Thank You)

www.ingramcontent.com/pod-product-compliance
Lightning Source LLC
Chambersburg PA
CBHW060952040426
42445CB00011B/1121